music of the romantic period

The tremendous growth and interest in basic music appreciation and literature courses and the increasing emphasis on music for the general college student demands fresh approaches to teaching and learning at the introductory level.

The Music Horizons Series represents a significant attempt to meet these needs by providing students with stimulating material of high quality by an authority in the field as well as providing instructors with the advantage of complete flexibility in organizing and teaching their course. Although the individual titles are self-contained, collectively they cover the full scope of music appreciation, literature and history.

music of the romantic period

Johannes Riedel
University of Minnesota

WM. C. BROWN COMPANY PUBLISHERS, *Dubuque, Iowa*

The Brown Music Horizons Series

Books now available

MUSIC IN THE UNITED STATES—*Arthur C. Edwards and W. Thomas Marrocco,* U.C.L.A.

MUSIC THROUGH THE RENAISSANCE—*James C. Thomson,* University of Kansas

THE CONCERTO—*Wendell Nelson,* University of California

MUSIC OF THE ROMANTIC PERIOD—*Johannes Riedel,* University of Minnesota

MUSIC OF THE CLASSIC PERIOD—*Theodore E. Heger,* University of Michigan

Consulting Editor
Frederick W. Westphal
Sacramento State College

Library of Congress Catalog Card Number: 69-12431

Printed in the United States of America

preface

The coming of the nineteenth century witnessed some very fundamental changes in music, changes which affected both the composer and his audience. Instead of the closed circle of the musically elite to which Haydn had addressed himself at Esterhazy, Beethoven found occasion in the finale of the *Ninth Symphony* to address "alle Menschen," or else to write, as it were, "for himself and his God—confessions of a solitary." Such precedents were eagerly subscribed to by his successors, who felt that they were catering to all humanity, limited neither by social stratification nor by national boundaries.

The general public responded to this change with genuine enthusiasm. Whereas it might have been more difficult to follow analytically the abstract compositions of the Classical era, presented as they were without further explication, the audience now found composers with works completely garnished with full critical analyses, theoretical apologia, and programmatic materials, including even the sources of inspiration, geneses, and realization—all by the primal authority, the composer himself. Even when not bidden to do so, this general audience seized upon the idea that the musical process could be patently verbalized, and that musical taste need not necessarily be cultivated by the old, tedious method of practice and craftsmanship, but by the direct method of intelligent reading of the authorities, later to be confirmed by the sound of the music itself. Furthermore, this process was made even more pleasurable by reinforcing democratic sentiments, along with tailoring subject material for dream fantasies during listening.

The purpose of this book is to make the general college student aware of the elements of change and expansion of the totality of music in a

Romantic world. The book is meant to be an aid and stimulation to those who might never have experienced the feeling for the wind which blew over the world in the nineteenth century. General rather than complete information, in combination with discussions of a cultural and sociological nature, is the goal of this volume. Certain omissions were thus made necessary. The discussion of musical nationalism, for instance, had to be limited to a few countries only. I hope that this will be understood by my readers.

JOHANNES RIEDEL

To
VANETT LAWLER

contents

part I

OVERVIEW OF THE NINETEENTH CENTURY

chapter 1

introduction: the social order and music

EXPANSION AND THE NINETEENTH CENTURY

Perhaps the most salient characteristic of the nineteenth century is the *continuous expansion* of nearly every facet of human life and progress within European civilization. Political and social currents stirred up by the French Revolutions of 1789, 1830, and 1848 were beginning to sweep aside old social institutions. In their stead middle-class society took over. With a hitherto unimaginable increase in productivity, a new order expanded to all parts of the globe and saturated all areas of material and artistic experience.

Nineteenth-century society witnessed an explosion of creativity, for instance, in the area of mechanical invention. The preceding century had furnished many basic inventions and the necessary laborsaving devices: Hargreaves' spinning jenny in 1767, Crompton's spinning mule in 1779, and Whitney's cotton gin in 1791. In the nineteenth century the number and productivity of inventors multiplied many times over. Transportation systems grew up in a very short time; within the first quarter of the century both the steam boat (1802) and the railroad (1825) appeared. Steel production, the electric light, food canning, the telephone and telegraph, electromagnetic induction, office machines, and machine tools were among the developments which were conceived and mass produced within this one century. Democratic large-scale applications of the new knowledge were undertaken at once; the first underseas cable was laid in 1851 between France and England, applying the very latest knowledge to the production of a modern communications system.

Although the nineteenth century was only the beginning of a fantastic technological progress which in our day has become commonplace, its impact upon society had grave consequences. The coming of the Industrial Revolution unquestionably made life very difficult for many kinds of workers for several decades. The concept of evolution, a theme developed in the writings of Charles Darwin, began to occur to many persons, both leaders and the "common" man. Furthermore, the concept that change can be natural and even useful—an idea also stressed by Darwin's theories—gradually found acceptance. The increased democratization of society and the need for more highly skilled workers made public education a necessity. Humanist and Rationalist thought, now newly tempered by the doctrines of Rousseau, turned philosophy toward a new direction of education, and a concept of widened horizons came into being. Through the efforts of Pestalozzi and his followers, the idea of mass education became a reality.

Another facet of nineteenth-century expansion is the increase of knowledge in the medical sciences and public health. Improved sanitation and drains, the availability of factory-made soap, and a ready market of cheap cotton clothes were but a few of the widely spread advances. The inception of the nursing profession and of the professionally trained pharmacist occurred simultaneously with the revolutionary appearance of anesthetics (especially ether and antiseptics). Research doctors, such as Pasteur, Lister, and Röntgen, made remarkable discoveries. Many diseases were wiped out, notably cholera, small pox, and bubonic plague, and with these advances came hope of conquering other serious diseases. An immediate result of these gains in health was an increased number of people. In Great Britain, for example, the population rose from 8 million in 1781 to 16 million in 1831; by 1901 the population had again doubled to 37 million. Every level of government felt the pressure of this population explosion. Among other indirect effects one may note the colonial expansion undertaken by nearly every European nation during the late nineteenth century. It is extremely significant in cultural history that colonialization brought an interchange of cultural ideas, an interchange greatly facilitated by the new, simpler, and quicker communications systems.

The Expanded Musical Audiences

The impact of these political, social, and industrial advances was immediately felt in musical life. Of primary importance is the fact that music reached a larger audience than at any other time in history. The newly-rich, newly-educated classes provided audiences in far greater numbers and percentages than the aristocratic, court-oriented classes had ever provided in the previous era. The history of nineteenth-century music cannot be told without reference as well to the history of its musical institutions. The music theaters with their financial and organizational backers, the concert societies with their membership enlistments, subscription concert devices, and other promotional procedures, the concert enterprises and agencies, entertainment halls, dance halls, and cabarets with their unique practices—all these flourished as a result of the broadened exposure of the public to more music and to materials related to music. The growing activity in music publishing and the promotion of music through cultural magazines, music periodicals, and columns devoted to music in daily newspapers increased rapidly.

With the increase in speed and ease of travel, concert life was extended into communities where it had been previously unknown. Performing musicians were able to travel extensively, and soon developed a taste for the nomadic life, the audience adulation, and the mounting recital fees. The recitals, in turn, stimulated music sales, and the publishing industry found and fostered an eager buying public. Instrument manufacturers, in turn, found a rapidly expanding market, particularly in the keyboard instruments, and they responded by applying new tooling and manufacturing devices to the increased production and improvement of their products. Both the publishing and instrument industries took advantage of the new promotional and marketing techniques and readily competed for the new markets. This, in turn, created more demand for teachers and performers alike, and the century saw the founding of great conservatories of music in every important city.

These expanded facilities and extended horizons were noted carefully by nineteenth-century artists. Composers and performers alike extended every effort to reach out to the ever-expanding audiences. The composer sought out substance both within and without his own personal experience, exploring "local color" subjects, the vernacular, wider ranges of timbres and ever larger orchestras, all designed to assist communication between the artist and his audience. Sensing in the tenor of contemporary life the problems that the machine age was creating and the tensions that the forces of rapid change were bringing into the daily lives of the citizenry, the composer turned to exotic and escapist material. Folklore furnished a wealth of colorful material with nostalgic overtones reinforced by nationalistic emotions. The artist explored the dream world, the supernatural, and various personal topics, all of which emphasized the human qualities that distinguish man as an individual. He also reacted against the mechanical world by exploring his propensities for objects of the natural world, for example, in things pertaining to night, and by establishing a personal closeness to religion.

trary, many leading musicians were assisted in various ways by this means.

Patronage took on new forms and dimension in the nineteenth century through the *salons* and *soirees* of middle-class Parisian society. In these circles, along with the fashionable virtuosi of the day, the "dime a dozen" composers and boudoir heroes typical of the time, however, brilliant personalities like those of Frederic Chopin (1810-1849) and Franz Liszt (1811-1886) are to be found.

While the aristocracy underwrote the complete expense of artists in the eighteenth century, the nineteenth-century patronage was assumed by the rich, newly-formed middle classes. The new patrons, by merely supplementing the artists' incomes, continued to exert some measure of influence upon the types of composition which the artists produced. Court-employed musicians during the Baroque and Classical eras naturally produced music for a musically literate clientele; they wrote specified music for specific events, with the choices of instrumentation, forms, vocal parts, and even lengths of the works decided largely by the resources of the court musical staff. By contrast, even when dependent to some degree on the financial assistance of patrons, nineteenth-century composers addressed a larger audience and were unusually free to compose what they pleased. In short, the nineteenth-century composer, even if he received direct economic aid, found that there were "fewer strings attached." This greater degree of artistic freedom can be illustrated by many examples. In Dresden, the banker Oppenheimer and the Mayor Serre performed chamber works of Karl Gottlieb Reissiger (1798-1859), not because Reissiger was obligated to compose these works specifically for them, but rather because these civic leaders enjoyed Reissiger's works and wished to help the artist by performing his compositions. Dvořák, upon the recommendation of Johannes Brahms (1833-1897), Eduard Hanslick (1825-1904), and Johann Herbeck (1831-1877), received a state stipend for four consecutive years for his continued endeavors. Dvořák was able to use the assistance as he chose and to compose as he pleased, so he was liberated by the patronage system rather than limited by it. Patronage was, indeed, frequently granted through the personal recommendation of leading musicians: Engelbert Humperdinck (1854-1921) was recommended by Richard Strauss (1864-1949) to the Krupp family, which sought in 1885 to employ a "*musikalischer Gesellschafter*" for their estate (Hagel).

There appeared a visible expression of change with the revolutionary currents which had gradually gained momentum during the eighteenth century, a change which may be described as an emancipation of the individual toward progressively greater degrees of political and social freedom. Until late in the eighteenth century, music reflected relatively little freedom from utilitarian purposes, for music was usually designed for specific church or court occasions. These works were written for immediate use, rather than being independent art works for the sake of art. At any rate, they certainly were not art for the sake of soul-sharing on the part of the composer. The gradual rise of public opera houses, first in Italy and then in Austria and Germany, brought a new focus upon audience demands. What had initially begun as private performances for very select groups gradually became an ostentatious luxury of an expanded group of aristocrats and *nouveau riches;* ultimately the opera house was to become the property of the general public. When in 1742 George Frideric Handel (1685-1759) produced *The Messiah,* he was making one of the first open bids for mass audience consumption disassociated from the luxury-oriented opera, and as such this oratorio has remained very dear to the public as if it were a symbol of that transformation.

Use of Folk Materials

Late Romantic composers expanded their materials still further than did their immediate predecessors. One of the ways in which this extension was made was through the use of folk materials of their native cultures. In their efforts to promote their individual cultures, composers such as Dvořák, Edvard Grieg (1843-1907), and the Russian Five drew upon folklore, often adapting melodies, melody types, patterns, and the choral folk music forms. The works of the Russian Five reflect the influence of the Byzantine, Oriental, and Russian cultures, particularly through the use of the whole tone scale. Grieg used the notes to which the age-old Norwegian Hardanger fiddle had been tuned for some of his compositions. In these ways folk materials stimulated art music in countries which had previously been of minor importance musically. This acceptance and promotion of folk materials was not only used as a link with the frequently exalted past, but was also evidence of a new dimension of nationalistic spirit in political life. It must be noted that composers were by no means the only persons interested in folk music; indeed, folk music societies sprang up in nearly every Western nation during the nineteenth century, often through the efforts of interested nonmusicians.

Suggested Reading Assignments

Cbt pp. 341-349
EaM pp. 1-72
FdA pp. 383-387
GdA pp. 492-500
Lpm pp. 719-725; 734-740; 801-809; 960-973
UhA pp. 426-428

chapter 2

musical materials of the romantic period

HARMONY AND KEY AREAS

Harmony, which in its general sense denotes the vertical structure of music, has specific aspects which need to be more clearly defined in order to understand the harmonic practice of the Romantic era. There is first of all the *harmony of key areas,* of which the most important are the major and minor modes. Both modes were used during the preceding Classic period, but composers reserved the minor key for specific expressive passages, and its use was the exception rather than the rule. Ludwig van Beethoven (1770-1827) first exploited the possibilities of the minor mode, particularly in his handling of c minor, which came to be known as the "tragic" key, just as C major became the "triumphant" key. Schubert, in his *Winterreise,* Op. 89, used the minor mode for sixteen songs, but the major for only eight.

This Romantic preference for the minor mode was paralleled by an increased tendency to use "distant" keys, a trend which became especially well-established in piano music. Beethoven's *Sonata,* Op. 78, for example, was in F-sharp major, Weber's Op. 39 in A-flat, and Chopin's Op. 58 in b minor. The search for new tonal possibilities, a part of the Romantic quest for the extraordinary and the fanciful, resulted in key relationships based on color rather than on function. This quest occupied composers for nearly a century before Béla Bartók (1881-1945), Arnold Schoenberg (1874-1951), and Igor Stravinsky (1882-   ) began explorations outside the major and minor systems.

An important aspect of the *harmony of key areas* lies in the relationship among the various movements in instrumental works. Beethoven's middle period works show a growing preference for key relationships at the interval of a third, and Schubert often wrote movements only a second apart. Wagner's operas show a final stage in the development of key relationships. These works are organized according to discernible key areas, which are closely connected with the opera's dramatic action and motivic layout.

CHROMATICISM AND ENHARMONICISM

The adoption of tempered tuning during the eighteenth century made possible two important developments in nineteenth-century harmonic practice: chromaticism and enharmonicism. Before the advent of tempered tuning, all tones bore a precise and simple mathematical ratio to the note selected as the tonal center. The tones of a harpsichord could, for example, be tuned in the correct ratios to the pitch of the note *A*. If a different pitch, however, were taken as the tonal center, most of the ratios would then be incorrect, and the instrument would be out of tune for the new tonal center or *tonic*. By adjusting the ratios, compromising or *tempering* the tuning, the instrument could be used with any pitch as the tonal center, i.e., any of the twelve tones of the octave could be used as the tonic. This is what we call chromaticism.

The effect of chromaticism can be observed by comparing the second theme of Schubert's *Symphony No. 8* ("Unfinished") with the *Prelude* to Wagner's *Tristan*. The Schubert melody, played by the cellos after a long note from the horn has interrupted the agitation of the first theme, expresses the simplicity of music without chromaticism. It is easy to sing—and, in fact, was once a popular song in this country. Compare this with the opening of Wagner's *Prelude*. Here is a melody begun by the same instruments and answered by the oboe. This melody is chromatic, moving step-wise through the twelve semitones of the octave. Instead of the security of the Schubert melody there is an atmosphere of complexity and of conflicting emotions. Although singable, it is hard to believe that this seemingly endless melody could ever become a popular song. The "endless" melody, one of Wagner's ideals, is made possible by chromaticism. The tonal center, which provided Schubert with such a strong base for starting and ending a melody, was weakened by chromaticism and eventually disappeared in the serial music of Schoenberg and others.

Enharmonicism is another aspect of chromaticism and amounts to this: just as one thing can have two names, e.g., "six of one or half a dozen of another," so can a note be called in one instance *f*-sharp and in another *g*-flat. Therefore, a final tone, let us say *f*-sharp which brings one melody to a close, can become, through changing relationships with other tones, *g*-flat and thus carry the melody to a new and different conclusion.

Listen to the Wagner *Prelude* again. After the third entrance of the cellos you hear the flute echo the oboe. Violins repeat the last two tones softly. The flute repeats these two tones. Then harmony under these tones shifts (relationships are changed) and the music moves on to a new melodic and emotional height. Enharmonicism thus supports the changes brought about by chromaticism. Enharmonicism became an important element in the thematic transformation of Liszt and in the development of the symphonic poem.

ORCHESTRATION IN THE EIGHTEENTH CENTURY

The expansion of the Romantic orchestra had its beginnings in the preceding century in both the addition of more players and new instruments. J. S. Bach's (1685-1750) Baroque orchestra numbered thirteen to sixteen players; by 1756 the Mannheim orchestra included forty-five to fifty players. Haydn expanded his orchestra only for the London symphonies where he was writing for a metropolitan symphony orchestra. Beethoven used a basic Mozart orchestra for most of his works, but in the *Ninth Symphony,* Op. 125, D minor, and the *Missa Solemnis,* Opus 123, D major, he introduced the bass clarinet, the English horn, and the contra-bassoon, thus crossing the boundary between Classical and Romantic orchestration.

ROMANTIC ORCHESTRATION

The Romantic orchestrator sought to discover the expressive qualities of instruments in order to use them effectively as an outlet for his own thought and sentiment. He considered the instrument in itself, its technical scope, its unique timbre, along with all of its other possibilities. With Romantic composers various instrumental timbres began to overlap. Schubert allowed horns to overlap bassoons; in other respects his orchestra is still a classical instrument, and only the string section functions as an independent choir. The woodwinds are blended with each other and occasionally with the strings, rather than being exploited for individual tone colors. As a result his orchestral palette is realized in pastels. Weber exploited the low ranges of all instruments—strings, woodwinds, and brasses—as a source of color and dramatic effect. Early Mendelssohn, Brahms, and Grieg followed the classical principle of instrumental distribution, but the late Mendelssohn, (as in the *Scotch*

Symphony, Op. 56, A minor-major), Schumann, and Liszt preferred the mixing of sounds of the different instrumental groups.

Mendelssohn

Mendelssohn's orchestration is the most Romantic aspect of his music. Careful listening to his *Overture* to Shakespeare's *Midsummer Night's Dream* will reveal the truth of this statement. The "magical" chords, which open the overture and within a space of five short bars set the atmosphere for the play, represent a Romantic use of the color of woodwinds, supported in the final chord by French horns. This is contrasted immediately with that of the higher strings. The typical Mendelssohn scherzo which follows is twice interrupted by woodwind chords reminiscent of the opening. The third interruption is a fortissimo entrance by the whole orchestra for sixteen bars, after which the strings, in rapid moving passages, are again contrasted with the sustained tones of the winds. Later, these roles are reversed.

The descending scales played *pizzicato* (plucked) by violins and cellos, which can be heard about midway in the overture, are another illustration of Mendelssohn's application of Romantic color to a Classic compositional device. Shortly after this the introductory chords are heard again, followed by a repetition of the scherzo which is now decorated with short and long notes from various wind instruments.

Although Mendelssohn's Romantic use of woodwind color is masterful, the most striking element of his orchestration lies in the demands he makes upon the string section. Each instrument is called upon for complete flexibility and a semi-virtuoso technic. Thus he makes the string section an expressive instrument, capable of portraying Romantic moods and pictures.

Berlioz

Giacomo Meyerbeer (1791-1864) and Berlioz were the first of the illustrious company of nineteenth-century orchestrators. Meyerbeer increased the number of players considerably, initiating a process of expansion that continued throughout the Romantic period. Perhaps the ultimate at this stage was achieved by Berlioz in the score for *Benvenuto Cellini*: two each of flutes, oboes, clarinets; four each of bassoons, horns, trumpets; two cornets, three trombones, tuba, tympani, cymbals, bass drum, triangle, thirty violins, ten violas, twelve violas, twelve cellos, nine basses, a total of ninety-three, two-thirds of which are strings.

One of the chief reasons Berlioz favored a large orchestra was the opportunity it gave to divide the sections of the orchestra according to his coloristic needs. Each of the string sections could thus be divided into full four-part harmony, creating new orchestral colors. Even the basses were sometimes divided as in the cantata, *The Fifth of May*. He seldom mixed timbres, but within each choir the instruments acquired new functions, often taking on new roles as solo instruments. The viola thus appears as soloist in *Harold in Italy,* Op. 16, a novel idea which reappears in Strauss's *Don Quixote,* Op. 35, at the end of the century.

Berlioz created the virtuoso orchestra. Jean-Baptiste Lully (1632-1687) and the Mannheim masters had developed the idea of a precision string body, and most of the Classic period was occupied with the realization of the full potentials of this instrument. It remained for Berlioz to initiate a similar development of the woodwind and brass ensembles. In his hands the players became not only a collection of performing virtuosi but a collective virtuoso instrument. In this way he regarded the orchestra in much the same way that Liszt regarded the piano and Niccolò Paganini (1782-1840) the violin.

Wagner

The Wagnerian orchestra represents a still further expansion. The larger orchestra gave Wagner, like Berlioz, the opportunity to subdivide any section. Thus, in the third act of *Lohengrin,* the violas are in four-part harmony, doubled by the violins. With *Lohengrin* a new conception of orchestration is revealed, concerned with the intimacy of single instrumental sounds and with combinations that produce an entirely new sound rather than the accumulation of instrumental sounds in terms of volume. Use of the bass clarinet forced the bassoon to the position of tenor and the clarinet to a higher pitch. Similarly, the horn quartet was moved to a higher position.

Wagner wanted the orchestra heard but not seen. At Bayreuth the orchestra pit was completely under the stage. In a sense it was like the swell box of an organ, fulfilling Wagner's intention that the orchestra should carry the harmony above which the melody could soar. The filled-out sections were ranks of pipes which he used like an organist, with the brass as a basic diapason tone. Even the strings served as harmonic instruments, sometimes reminding one of organ mixtures in their sound.

One of the greatest contributions of Romanticism was the development of the brass section, partly due to the role of brass bands in the life of the people. The orchestral role of brass instruments was expanded from the simple function of adding dynamic weight in *tutti* passages and injecting the outdoor vitality of the military fanfare. Just as the masses won a place in nineteenth-century society, so the brasses finally achieved full acceptance into the aristocratic circle of strings and woodwinds. In the music of Brahms and Bruckner (1824-1896) they acquired a refinement which was only matched but not surpassed in the impressionistic music of Claude Debussy (1862-1918) and his followers. It remained only for the American jazz virtuoso to complete the development of technical perfection in performance.

Rimsky-Korsakov

One of the greatest masters of orchestration *per se* was Nicolas Rimsky-Korsakov (1844-1908). An examination of his *Scheherazade*, Op. 35, brings to light many evidences of this mastery.

Only eight bars after the opening we are struck by a series of five woodwind chords which inevitably recall the beginning of Mendelssohn's *Midsummer Night's Dream Overture*. But there the similarity ends. We are immediately presented with a sensuous violin solo, accompanied by a single harp, an instrument which had no place in Mendelssohn's orchestra. Especially striking, at the end of the violin solo, is the richness and power of the enlarged cello section which Rimsky-Korsakov took for granted. He masses all the violins in a unison melody to dominate this heavy background. Later, oboes and clarinets are added to the melody to balance it against the sustained trombone harmony added to the cellos. As the intensity of the music mounts, the role of the brass section becomes increasingly important.

Later movements have effective, idiomatic solos for various instruments. Other features of the orchestration easily identified are the repeated *pizzicato* chords during the clarinet and bassoon cadenzas in the second movement, the many harp glissandos in the last movement, and the brilliant use of percussion instruments throughout most of the suite.

Rimsky-Korsakov, although quite capable of writing effectively for the whole orchestra, or any portion thereof, delighted more than most composers in providing real cadenza-like solos for practically every instrument. From one point of view this represents the last struggle of the individual virtuoso player to free himself from the mass domination of the huge Romantic orchestra, a struggle which, regrettably, was doomed to failure.

Suggested Listening Assignments

1. Schubert, Franz: *Symphony No. 8* (Unfinished). Listen for Schubert's melodic simplicity in the first movement. Can you sing all the melodies? Are they lyrical in expression?
2. Wagner, Richard: *Tristan and Isolde Prelude*. Listen for chromatic progressions. Do they occur all the time, at the beginning, or at the end of the musical statement? Is it easier to sing a melody with chromatic tones?

3. MENDELSSOHN, FELIX: *Midsummer Night's Dream Overture,* Opus 21. What role does the string section play in this overture? Does it blend well with other instruments or does it form a contrast easily detected?

SUGGESTED ADDITIONAL LISTENING ASSIGNMENTS

1. BERLIOZ, HECTOR: *Benvenuto Cellini Overture.* Can you make out which role each of the sections of the orchestra play in this music?
2. RIMSKY-KORSAKOV, NICOLAS: *Scheherazade,* Opus 35. How does the composer handle orchestral color? Look for examples of specific instruments.

SUGGESTED READING ASSIGNMENTS

CbT pp. 364-375; 462-465
EaM pp. 32-36
GdA pp. 535-537
HaM pp. 766-768; 752-758; 873-875
ScO pp. 267-272; 284-286

SUGGESTED WRITTEN ASSIGNMENTS

1. Take the first movement of any piano sonata or symphony by Beethoven, Schubert or Brahms. Trace how the composer moves from one key area to the next.
2. Write a short history of one single orchestral instrument.
3. Compare the scores of a Haydn symphony, a Schumann symphony, and a Wagner opera overture. List the instruments used by each composer. Describe the expansion of instruments in all sections of the orchestra.

FOOTNOTES

[1]LaD
[2]SjR, p. 71; MhG, p. 256
[3]MhG, p. 113
[4]SjR, p. 49
[5]SjR, p. 50
[6]SjR, p. 54
[7]SjR, p. 56
[8]SjR, p. 56

part II

MUSICAL FORMS

chapter 3

the sonata form

BEETHOVEN AND BRAHMS COMPARED

Vienna was the adopted home of both Beethoven and Brahms. Beethoven resided there in the early years of the Romantic period, and Brahms during the very height of that period's most luxuriant flowering. Thus, Beethoven's music began with a *style* disciplined by study and emulation of the Classic masters and ended, in his later years, in a highly personalized expression. Brahms, presenting a nearly opposite pattern in his life, began with a highly subjective approach, in the manner of Schumann, and moved consistently closer to an objective and formalistic style with the passing of the years. Both composers worked in the fields of piano music, chamber music, and symphonic works, with additional masterworks in large symphonic-choral media, and although Brahms's art songs are perhaps better known, Beethoven created many no less deserving, (such as the *Adelaide,* Opus 46).

From his mentor Schumann, Brahms learned an early reverence for Beethoven's symphonism. Other composers had been quick to elaborate upon the experimental aspects of Beethoven's works, and their efforts soon established such procedures as the norm. Brahms, however, preferred to keep his eye upon the older master's total consciousness of form and the techniques that made it functional even during the boldest strokes of harmonic, thematic, and formal experimentation. For the sake of this study, Brahms delayed production of the First Symphony, Opus 68, C minor, until after his fortieth year. Music criticism was quick to recognize superficial signs of his study of Beethoven and accused him of "having kidnapped the theme of his finale from Beethoven's Choral

Symphony, considering it the 'Tenth Symphony'—Brahms having taken up Beethoven's work." Brahms had indeed taken up Beethoven's work, but in a most idealistic and conscientious manner, and not in the derogatory sense intended by the critics. It was not only in the symphonic field that Brahms sought to emulate Beethoven, but also in the field of chamber music; the end of the first section of the trio in the Sextet in B-flat, Op. 18, for instance, rather strikingly recalls the corresponding trio section of Beethoven's Fifth Symphony, Opus 67, C minor.

Beethoven

The sonata form (or sonata-allegro) of Beethoven's early works, (Opus 1 to appr. Opus 35), is a three-sectioned movement founded upon principles of contrasted themes and changes of key. In Beethoven's hands the sonata form was in little danger of becoming a static set piece. His penchant for motivic development soon involved him in expansion far beyond the limits of his models in Haydn and Mozart, particularly in the development section, the coda, and the key changes of the exposition and recapitulation. These expansions were not just the symptoms of exuberance of youth or the excesses of a new Romanticism, but were the outward evidences of his growth as a composer, that in retrospect appears almost to have been planned and singularly purposive. That development shows a steady progress toward a basic unity of function and purpose for all elements of a composition: themes, rhythms, harmonies, and timbres. In Beethoven's early works he structured this unification around the realization of patterned abstractions in the classical forms, a patterning which soon assumed proportions of a *style*, characterized by unusual inventiveness and aggressive individuality. His working notebooks testify to his meticulous care in the selection or rejection of thematic possibilities according to their suitability to the individual composition. Essentially, this view of craftsmanship was "classical" in its outlook upon structure, except that its consistent rejection of commonplace formulae for more individualistic ones began to give it a coloring not readily associated with classical objectivity. With the passing of the years, increasing awareness of the force of his own personality and the dramatic possibilities achievable in the sonata-allegro and theme and variations forms led him to more personalized utterances. Ultimately, this led to associative extra-musical conceptions which dictated overriding ideas concerning dramatic formal structure. To these expressive ideas he bent the full strength of his will, and created a new flexibility within the classical forms that was essentially Romantic in its point of departure.

the thematic motive

The most fundamental element of Beethoven's style and approach to form is that of the *thematic motive.* Even in his earliest compositions, Beethoven showed a comprehensive grasp of the possibilities inherent in simple motivic units such as an interval, a rhythm, or a short harmonic sequence. The whole first movement of the *First Symphony,* Opus 21, C major, can be demonstrated as being founded upon a single harmonic relationship stated in the opening chords of the Introduction—a dominant seventh chord (on the tonic note, C) resolving to an F major chord. This unorthodox beginning achieved an immediate sense of tension which is seconded by the next set of chords, a G dominant leading (by regressive motion) to an a minor chord, and a third set, D dominant leading to G major. These three bold strokes establish the leading tone as a melodic force (E to F, then B to C, then F♯ to G) and clearly associate them with dominants and their resolutions (C to F, G to a, D to G). Beethoven then introduces this tension-producing complex into the first subject:

Example 1. Beethoven, *Symphony No. 1,* First Movement, Measures 13-17.

Part 1 of this subject reflects the dominant to tonic relationship and presents the leading tone in a new and more vigorous rhythmic version. Part 2 of the subject is a new rhythmic version of part 1, providing still further reinforcement of the established tensions and additional forward motion. Part 3 of the subject is a deliberate staccato march straight up through the tonic chord—with, of course, the leading tone prominantly displayed, E, G, B, C. This is followed by a new dominant-tonic chord statement (A dominant to d minor) part 4 in a new mode and key—significantly higher (on the supertonic of the original key) and thus rising in tension on the harmonic scale. The bridge passage which follows is likewise constructed of the same elements:

Example 2. Beethoven, *Symphony No. 1,* First Movement, Measures 37-38.

Example 3. Beethoven, *Symphony No. 1,* First Movement, Measures 41-43.

The second subject is founded upon the harmonies of measures 2, 3, and 4 of the Introduction (the beginning chord being reduced from a seventh chord to a plain triad) carrying on the same harmonic tensions, but now smoothed over by interlocking downward gliding phrases:

Example 4. Beethoven, *Symphony No. 1,* First Movement, Measures 53-57.

The development and recapitulation carry forward the same closely-knit structure, further exploring the possibilities of dominant-tonic relationships. Analysis of the other movements reveals the same economy of structure. The third movement has a scale-passage subject made of two components of the dominant-leading tone-tonic motive and a third component very nearly like it:

Example 5. Beethoven, *Symphony No. 1,* Third Movement, Measures 1-8.

Likewise, the figurations of the trio incorporate the same motive:

Example 6. Beethoven, *Symphony No. 1,* Third Movement (trio), Measures 85-86.

rhythm

Another very prominent feature of Beethoven's style is his use of rhythm. Treatment of the *sforzando,* particularly on weak beats, is so commonly recognized and commented upon as to have become a sort of trademark. Indeed, such passages as the one containing the famous dissonances in the development of the first movement of the "Eroica," Opus 55, Symphony No. 3 E-flat major, (measures 248 to 284), have the very pulsation stridency that even a full century later made Stravinsky's "Rite of Spring" (1913) shocking. Nevertheless, despite its importance in Beethoven's style, the *sforzando* is only one device in a framework of writing that is always vitally alive and abounding in much more subtle uses of rhythmic energy. There is, for instance, the opening of the *Scherzo* in the "Eroica," which sets up a diabolically furious pace, and then compounds it with continually displaced two-note patterns:

Example 7. Beethoven, *Symphony No. 3*, Scherzo Movement, Measures 1-3.

The subject of the *Grosse Fuge,* Op. 133, furnishes another example of accent displacement resulting in a display of rhythmic energy. The beginning notes of the fugue enter on the second beat of the measure. Taken alone this is not remarkable, but at the proper tempo and combined with the dotted rhythms of the countersubject, the second beat entry becomes a syncopation which the composer obviously took great delight in exposing to view.

Another vital factor in Beethoven's rhythmic style is his capacity for expansion and contraction of basic rhythmic patterns. At the beginning of the development is the first movement of the *Fourth Symphony,* Opus 60, B-flat major; successive parts of a four-bar sequence are broken into units of two bars (measures 206 to 222) and thereafter into one-bar units (to measure 234) before being released for full statement of the subject. In other instances, Beethoven used a rhythmic pattern to achieve in the *Fifth Symphony* where the famous "Fate knocking" motive of the first movement furnishes repeated-note patterns that constantly reappear in the remainder of the symphony. Not only do these repetitions and variants provide unity for the work, they also furnish much of the contrasting materials.

Example 8. Beethoven, *Symphony No. 5,* First Movement, Measures 1-2.

Brahms

Brahms based his style upon a coalition of two of the great strengths he observed in Beethoven's scores—variation and motivic development. There is evidence that he particularly studied the scores of the 32 variations on an original theme, Opus 191, c minor, and Diabelli, Opus 120, piano variations, the finale of the "Eroica," the adagio of the *Ninth Symphony,* and movements from the last period string quartets. Up until the last period works, Beethoven tended always to retain the "set piece" formation of his variations, each variant retaining the simple song form with the same number of measures. Correspondingly, he tended to reserve developmental techniques for the sonata form. In the last period works, however, Beethoven began to take more freedom with individual variations, particularly with those variations toward the conclusion of the set, as in the piano sonatas, Op. 109 and 111. For instance, in Op. 111, variation 4 is really two statements, the first quite regular with repeats written out, and the second free and developmental in nature. Variation 5 starts in a very regular way, but after the double bar it assumes almost a free fantasy. Brahms observed these techniques most closely, and from his observations evolved a highly personal style that was basically very dependent upon variations for structural articulation of form.

In Brahms's Opus 1, the first and second subjects and closing theme of the first movement and the first and second subjects of the finale are all drawn from the same motivic core phrase. An even more brilliant example is in the first movement of the Sonata, Op. 5; the thematic transformations are:

Example 9. Brahms, *Sonata,* First Movement, Measure 1.

Example 10. Brahms, *Sonata,* First Movement, Measure 7.

Example 11. Brahms, *Sonata,* First Movement, Measure 17.

Example 12. Brahms, *Sonata,* First Movement, Measures 23-24.

Example 13. Brahms, *Sonata,* First Movement, Measures 39-42.

Example 14. Brahms, *Sonata,* First Movement, Measures 56-58.

Furthermore, each of these forms a distinct variation period, many of which end with a distinct pause:

Example (1)	Measures	1 to 6
Example (2)	Measures	7 to 11
	Measures	12 to 16
Example (3)	Measures	16 to 22
Example (4)	Measures	23 to 30
	Measures	31 to 38
Example (5)	Measures	39 to 50
Example (6)	Measures	56 to 61
	(Repeat)	62 to 68

Measures 51 to 56 are occupied with a developmental episode founded upon the rhythm and harmony of the accompaniment of measure 51—a case of thematic growth out of a variation to the point where it no longer resembles the original theme at all.

Brahms's more mature compositions conceal this kind of formation, yet the variation principle is operable. The first movement of the *Fourth Symphony,* Opus 98, E minor, is a good case in point. The first subject is made up of two-note motives so charmingly strung together that they alone serve as an excellent example of the classic balance which Brahms strove for—each successive pair balances its predecessor perfectly in direction, harmony, and melodic continuity.

Example 15. Brahms, *Symphony No. 4,* First Movement, Measures 1-4.

At the same time, the theme is a core unit for the following variants in the exposition alone:

Example 16. Brahms, *Symphony No. 4,* First Movement, Measures 9-11.

Example 17. Brahms, *Symphony No. 4,* First Movement, Measures 13-17.

The exposition reveals the following variation-like formations:

(1) Measures 1 to 18
(2) Measures 19 to 44
(3) Measures 45 to 53
(4) Measures 53 to 87
(5) Measures 87 to 119
(6) Measures 119 to 136
(7) Measures 136 to 144

Yet all requisites are met for the sonata-allegro; everything moves as if the sonata structure were the only objective. The variation basis is only partially betrayed to the ear, except by a certain episodic nature that one seldom meets for example in Beethoven.

The full range of Brahms's versatility in variation techniques can best be seen in the finale of the *Fourth Symphony.* This movement is cast in the form of a passacaglia, a form that by its very nature, being based upon a repeated eight-measure theme, could tend to become something very static. Yet Brahms created the very opposite, and with all due classic methodology, produces a most powerful and impressive piece of dramatic Romanticism. The Classical aspect is reflected in the very stringent adherence to the original theme, which can be traced note for note in each of the thirty variations, sometimes undisguisedly near the surface, and at other times buried deeply in a texture of wholly dissimilar elements:

Example 18. Brahms, *Symphony No. 4,* Fourth Movement, Measures 1-8.

The variational devices come from the Classical inventory: inversions (Vars. 5 and 6), canon (30), points of imitation (2 and 13), decorative figurations (8 and 9), aria "on a ground" (12), and a consistent polyphonic texture. The Romantic aspects show in the lavishness of detail and the prodigious wealth of rhythmic, instrumental, contrapuntal, and harmonic devices. The harmonic texture, especially, is exhaustively Romantic. Brahms exposes every possible implication in the theme, particularly those suggested by the chromaticism A-A♯-B at the apex of the phrase, and these chromaticisms permeate the melodic line as well as the structural progressions. Each variation has a new harmonic detail, a new melodic device, or a new rhythmic idea, and this lucid individuality associates it with Romantic ideals. Every variation is a completely new creation, resembling no other in this or any other set, and only when one realizes the extent of this uniqueness is their seven-league distance from baroque "division" and rococo ornamentation fully evident.

The plotting of dramatic suspense is most remarkable. After the first group on nine momentum-gathering statements, there is a kind of "slow movement" of six meditative variations, the last three of which are significantly the only variations which turn to the parallel major key from the otherwise exclusively minor mode. With variation sixteen, Brahms returns to the theme, as if to refresh his memory of it, or to wipe away the digressiveness of the major key. Strings enter half way through number sixteen, impatient to move forward, and from this point onward the composition moves steadily toward a climax. In one sense, this is a recapitulation, for many of the variations duplicate the general nature of some of the first group, but in each case the variant is a complete reworking with consciously more aggressive tension added.

After variation thirty and a *poco ritardando* (the only tempo change except for the switch to 3/2 in vars. 12, 13, and 14), the music spills over into a Coda, *piu allegro.* Here, the theme is no longer given in its entirety, and the first real modulations in the whole composition take place, diminutions of the first five notes of the theme figuring prominently in bringing the whole to a close.

Diagrammatically, the structure is:

First Section	*Third Section*
Theme and 1	16 and 17, like Theme and 1
2 and 3	18, 19 and 20, like 2 and 3
4, 5, and 6	
7	21 totally new
8 and 9	22 and 23, like 8 and 9
"Slow Movement"	
	24 and 25, like 1 and 2
Second Section	26 and 27, like 3 and 5
10, 11, 12	28, 29, 20 New
13, 14, and 15 Major Key	*Coda* (57 measures)

The essential unity of this composition no doubt springs from the repeated germinal theme, yet the impression is not one of unity by repetition but rather of a unity by diversity. In it, musical events occur with the same logic as that of a well-told narrative. It is a somber narrative, and perhaps this is its greatest point of unity—a mood of consistent gravity that can shift from shades of melancholy to tones of grief without once losing its calm self-possession.

Suggested Listening Assignments

1. Beethoven, Ludwig van: *Symphony No. 1,* Opus 21. In what ways does the composer achieve musical unity? How are the elements of motivic repetition, variation, and contrast handled in the first movement?
2. Beethoven, Ludwig van: *Symphony No. 5,* Opus 67. In what ways are the elements of rhythmic repetition, variation, and contrast handled? What role does syncopation and heavy accent play in the first movement?
3. Brahms, Johannes: *Sonata,* Opus 1. Observe the thematic transformations in the first movement.
4. Brahms, Johannes: *Symphony No. 4,* Opus 98. Listen for the passacaglia form as explained in the text.

Suggested Additional Listening Assignments

1. Beethoven, Ludwig van: *Symphony No. 3,* Opus 55. How is rhythm treated in the Scherzo? Do you find any long melodies? Does the orchestration reinforce the rhythmic movement?

2. BEETHOVEN, LUDWIG VAN: *Symphony No. 4*, Opus 60. Listen to the technique of motivic-rhythmic contraction in the development section of the first movement.

SUGGESTED READING ASSIGNMENTS

CbT pp. 329-340; 403-408
EaM pp. 81-85; 149-154
FdA pp. 334-341; 363-382; 499-513
GdA pp. 470-491; 539-542
HaM pp. 631-658; 693-703
LpM pp. 750-776; 895-904
ScO pp. 255-260; 300-302
UhA pp. 404-424; 480-488

SUGGESTED WRITTEN ASSIGNMENTS

1. Compare the themes used by Beethoven in any one of the symphonies discussed in this chapter as to key, form, tempo, length.
2. Check on the variation form as treated by Beethoven in his 32 *Variations on an Original Theme*, Opus 191, or the *Diabelli Variations*, Opus 120.
3. Describe the kind of rhythms you hear in Beethoven's *Ninth Symphony*.

chapter 4

the art song: schubert

HISTORICAL BACKGROUND

Franz Schubert, perhaps the greatest song composer in the history of music, literally changed the face and direction of nineteenth-century song literature. Figuratively, then, he is referred to as "the father of the lied," but since the German lied had been cultivated for many centuries before Schubert, it is necessary for us to take a brief look at that history in order to understand the nature of his contribution.

The German solo song has a long ancestry extending back through the Mastersingers and the Minnesingers. French influences, through the Troubadors, are believed to have sparked the first Minnesinger compositions, and its art flourished until the end of the thirteenth century, when it was largely taken over by the Meistersingers. German solo song, however, was generally hindered in its development by a lack of truly great poetry.

On the musical side, a true German *Lied* was imperiled by the persistent influence of the Italian style which maintained a strong hold in the important musical centers during the whole of the Baroque period. The Italian *cantilena* seemed to strike no real affinities with the German language. Eventually there was a sharp reaction against these influences in Rationalistic North Germany, a reaction of severe artistic simplicity that was self-defeating and strangely persistent. The principal composer in the North German style, Johann Friedrich Reichardt (1752-1814), occasionally indulged in declamatory experiments, and demonstrated that an accompaniment could be made picturesque such as by suggesting a brook rippling over pebbles, or made variable by minor colorings in succeeding strophes. However, these experiments proved unsuccessful for the most part, and Reichardt had his greatest success in the simple strophic form in which he generally composed.

North German ideas came to be checked, on the other hand, by Austrian composers, whose vocal works retained a high degree of Italianate influences. Even with composers like Haydn and Mozart, the poetry was kept subordinated to the music, and though both made settings of some great poetry (Shakespeare and Goethe), they fostered no real song tradition. During this same period, the *Lied* was being influenced by a newer artistic type, the genuine melodrama (not to be confused with a late Romantic dramatic form) in which the spoken word, usually an emotional monologue, was given an orchestral background in the manner of a *recitativo accompagnato.* The accompanying orchestra reflected and heightened the prevailing emotion and provided scenic backgrounds of sunrises, pastoral settings, thunderstorms, or tempests. Out of this combination of melodrama and song came still another form, the ballad, and it was this new genre that began to show the true Romantic traits. It was Johann Rudolf Zumsteeg (1760-1802) of Stuttgart who was the first great exponent of this form, and whose strophic songs and short ballads made a strong impression upon Schubert.

MUSIC, POETRY, AND THE LIED

One matter which cannot be overlooked in regard to influences upon Schubert is his unique and singularly fortunate historical position, for he happened to be born into one of the greatest periods in German literature. German song would no longer be hindered by a lack of inspirational poetry. Not only did Schubert inherit the tradition of Klopstock and Hölty, but he became a younger contemporary of Goethe and Schiller. Furthermore, he lived through the expansion of the Romantic movement in poetry—with Tieck, the Schlegel brothers, Novalis, and Heinrich Heine. In addition, Ossian, Petrarch, Walter Scott, and Shakespeare were made available to him through excellent translations—also a product of the Romantic era.

As significant as the new infusion of worthwhile poetry was the development of a new concept of the relationship of words and music. By Schubert's time, poetry had assumed an importance far greater than it had ever known. The poet, having been one of the first to announce the tenets of Romantic esthetic ideals, was now somewhat in the position of arbiter of taste. (Many even saw the poet as prophet of the future; thus it is easy to see why the lied reached its apex in the early Romantic era.) Composers were forced to recognize the need to give expression to the new poetic concepts made available to them, and a more sympathetic approach to the demands of the text appeared in opera, oratorio, and cantata, as well as in the *Lied*. No doubt part of Schubert's greatness lies in the fact that he recognized the new order of things, and, having accepted this new relationship between poet and musician, was far more creative in a purely musical sense than any previous song writer. It should be clearly recognized that Schubert did not carry this new relationship to the opposite extreme. Had he done so, and treated the poetry as absolutely supreme, he would not have created the careful balance of forces that made him the "father of the *Lied*." That balance between musical and poetic elements raised harmony, rhythm, and accompaniment to equal importance with the text and the melody. ("He brought to bear upon the atmosphere of the song the force of an overwhelming musical organism, a force sufficient to establish a balance between poetry and music.")[1] Paradoxically, the melodies of Schubert's songs can be sung unaccompanied without losing their integrity. Likewise, the accompaniments hold to their own musical consistency, keeping the mood and background while the voice fills in the detail. In fact, the piano accompaniment has enough homogeneity to make a kind of composition of its own, a kind of character piece; Liszt's transcriptions bear this out. Yet, for all this independence of components, text and music in a Schubert song unite to make a whole.

According to Arthur Hutchings, Schubert had a very definite taste in verse but it was the taste of a songster, not of a philosopher or literary esthete.[2] Knowing just what kinds of verse suggest musical expression, he chose 71 out of 603 songs with Goethe texts. Perhaps this was completely by instinct, or perhaps by some very positive standards which he never bothered to state. It is also worthy of note that Schubert was born into the literate, but by no means urbane middle class. Other composers had tended to rise, at least by association, to the upper classes. Schubert preferred to remain closer to the peasantry, and he evidently wished to live in a more intimate, congenial, and decidedly less socially-conscious atmosphere. However, it is impossible to conclude that Schubert was entirely lacking in critical literary judgment, for it is still possible, even today, for singers to fully appreciate the literary side of these songs and to gain pleasure from joining with the composer in recreating its musical quality. Indeed, there is no need for the singer to close off half his intelligence to sing songs like *Der Doppelgänger* (1828) or *Gretchen am Spinnrade,* Opus 2. Since Schubert's time, no song composer of any stature has dared to be without a literary conscience. Whether this was due entirely to Schubert or was one of the definite heritages of the Romantic era in general can never be determined for sure, but we may be certain that Schubert was a primary agent of its inception.

SCHUBERT'S MELODIC GIFT

If one had to choose one particular characteristic in the whole of Schubert's song style as being the most salient and arresting, this choice would without any doubt have to be Schubert's melodic inventiveness. Perhaps never before or since has there been a composer who has even begun to match Schubert's amazing spontaneity, originality, and amplitude in melody. This melodic gift, which was often responsible for the destruction of form in his sonatas and symphonies, turns out now to be the greatest strength in his song style. In the course of writing over six hundred songs, Schubert hardly ever repeated himself melodically.

Much of the charm and spontaneity of Schubert's melody is due to his constant search for variety, and nowhere is this more apparent than in his flexible and unobtrusive handling of phrasing. In general, he followed the example of his Classical heritage, which traditionally set its basic periods by observing the poetic stanza in lines of four-bar periods. This basic pattern underlies the whole of Schubert's song structures, although a perfectly square period of symmetrical four-bar components is rather rare. The song, *Wohin*?, Opus 25 (*Die Schöne Müllerin*), for example, is on such. Schubert tried for the most part to avoid this squareness either by extending or shortening the phrase length. The simplest device is to echo the vocal lines (e.g. *Taubenpost*). Another, and by far the most frequently used device, is to echo the vocal cadence in the piano accompaniment. As a matter of fact, Schubert used this device so often that it may almost be considered a mannerism.[3] Frequently, however, the echo effect plays an important role in the poetic or psychological import of the poem, and in these cases becomes one of the most haunting of musical effects (e.g. *Der Doppelgänger*). A third and very frequent device is the extension of the phrase by only a measure or even a half-measure, usually in the piano prelude or interlude. An excellent example of this is seen in the prelude to *Frühlingsglaube*, Opus 20, #2 (1820), where a half-bar extension in measure four forces a five bar period.

Example 1. Schubert, *Frühlingsglaube*, Measures 1-5.

SCHUBERT'S LIED FORMS

Schubert used two general forms for his songs, the strophic and the through-composed. Both of these must be considered as a very general type for they are treated with a good deal of freedom and variety with no formalized pattern. The origin of the strophic song can be found in folk song, while the origin of the continuous through-composed form is most directly traceable through the operatic *scena.* Superficially the difference between the two is that of stanzaic as opposed to blank verse construction.

The through-composed is generally the more dramatic of the two forms in almost every respect. Schubert treated these the most freely, in some cases so freely as to make it difficult to analyze. In every case, however, the freedoms spring from actual demands of the text. There are a few generalized types:

1. Strictly through-composed, no repetitions, no marked division.
2. Those broken into mood or narrative sections.
3. Recitative and aria, arioso formations.
4. Those with alternated recitative-like or declamatory passages with cantabile or lyrical passages.
5. Short songs in recitative or declamatory style.

Usually the through-composed songs are musical paintings, planned in a broad, dramatic, cantata-like manner in which the pictorial element plays a large role. The joy of illustration is carried to such lengths in this form that every definitely marked text-picture is rendered with its specific tone-painting—most often in the piano accompaniment, but not infrequently in the voice part itself. Unity is supplied through some specific devices, the most characteristic being a specific motive in the accompaniment which is repeated at critical points in the composition. This device became very popular during the course of the Romantic era, and many composers used it on a large scale in operatic and symphonic genres as well as in the art song, e.g. Berlioz's *idée fixe* and Wagner's *Leitmotiv.* Schubert, however, recognized other unifying possibilities and employed devices such as short recurring motives in the voice or, interestingly enough, recurring harmonic ostinatos (*Der Doppelgänger*). The melodic types in these songs would be called recitative or dramatic lyrical arioso. Setting certain poems in this genre proved to be a most ambitious undertaking, as for example with Schiller's *Der Taucher* (1814).

The strophic songs are definitely more lyrical than the through-composed and they also show a great deal of variety. Many are in a rather strict strophic form, in which a set of stanzas is set to identical repetitions of the same melody, e.g. *Heidenröslein,* Opus 3, #3 *Wo ist*

Sylvia? Opus 106, #4. There are many Lieder representing the first stage of "modified strophic form," in which the song is divided into two parts, the second being a repetition of the first with small but very significant modifications, e.g. *Greisengesang.* In all cases the modifications appear in response to specific demands of the texts. Clearly, Schubert's artistic aim in writing the strophic song was to achieve a compression of material. What he has done in the strophic song, and most specifically in the strict strophic type, is to abstract a central theme or mood from the entire poem, to translate it into music for the voice and accompaniment, and then to let this music stand unchanged for all strophes. As more variations and mutations appear in the form in the interest of heightened color, drama, or illustration, we can see the influence of the through-composed song asserting itself, and, in the process, changing the face of the strophic song quite radically. The final result is represented in songs like *Heiss mich nicht reden* (1826), setting in e minor, where the second stanza is treated differently from the first and the music of the third makes no more than a passing reference to the first. In such a case the two forms, strophic and through-composed, have virtually been merged.

THE BALANCE OF VOICE AND ACCOMPANIMENT

Schubert, like Beethoven, was able to make significant innovations in his accompaniments because of the recent improvements in the pianoforte. The new instrument was immediately responsive to touch, could produce either a smooth cantabile or a curt staccato, had a new resonance in chordal and pedal effects, and offered an infinitely varied range of color possibilities. *An mein Klavier* (1816), Schubert's tribute to the piano, features resonant, mellow sustained chords, and repeated chords—impossible choices for the generation before him. In comparison with the present day piano, this instrument was rather thin in tone, but the treble was warm and mellow, explaining why the piano parts of Schubert's songs lie almost exclusively within a wide middle register.

Older ideas of accompaniments are reflected in the words of Goethe, who said "the accompaniment be handled with great moderation, since in moderation alone there is richness." From this alone one can see why Goethe preferred Carl F. Zelter's (1758-1832) pale settings to Schubert's, whose songs virtually represent the opposite extreme of this view. Often these accompaniments are actually more elaborate and virtuosic in nature than the voice parts themselves, and publishers even complained to Schubert about their difficulty. Actually, with Schubert the word "accompaniment" is permanently retired because both piano and voice became protagonists in a drama of self-realization. In the Schubert song both the psychologically expressive and the tonally pictorial are molded into a whole with no sharp lines of demarcation as to specific functions for the two. Since the pictorial elements were usually assigned to the piano, it must be pointed out that Schubert did not simply revel in empty reproduction of natural sounds. He certainly did not shun representational elements when they suited a particular artistic purpose but, for the most part, the relationship between Schubert's musical expression and the representational element is simply the poetic idea they share in common.

One important structural element, the prelude, is entrusted to the piano alone. In his earlier songs, Schubert often omitted a piano introduction, but in the later songs the introduction came to be crucial to the song itself. Then, when publishing an old song, Schubert would invariably compose an introduction to go with it. There were good reasons for this preference. First of all, the introduction established the mood and atmosphere of the piece so that words would not be lost in creating background. The prelude also established the key, and Schubert apparently preferred to establish the tonic by a full anticipatory phrase. And, finally, he anticipated the piano figuration to come, something of the melodic outline or future harmonic colors, and not infrequently, some of the later events of the song.

Suggested Listening Assignments

1. Schubert, Franz: *Die schöne Müllerin.* These songs form a cycle, a continuous story of youth and love. In what ways are the songs knit together? What are the similarities between the songs?
2. Schubert, Franz: *Heidenröslein.* What does the folk-song quality of this art song consist of? What is its basic form? What is the relationship between the piano and the vocal part?
3. Schubert, Franz: *Der Erlkönig.* Listen for this song's through-composed structure. Become aware of the close relationship between the action of the poem, the accompaniment, and the melodic treatment.

Suggested Additional Listening Assignments

1. Schubert, Franz: *Schwanengesang.* What is the primordial emotional quality in these songs? What do songs such as *Die Stadt, Am Meer, Der Doppelgänger* have in common?
2. Schumann, Robert: *Frauenliebe und-leben.* What are the similarities between the different songs? In what ways does Schumann differ from Schubert?
3. Wolf, Hugo: *Spanisches Liederbuch.* What is the relationship between the piano and the vocal part? Listen for some specific chromatic successions and relate them to the text.

Suggested Reading Assignments

CbT pp. 349-356
EaM pp. 86-101
FdA pp. 387-400
GdA pp. 500-503
HaM pp. 659-669
LpM pp. 776-786
ScO pp. 263-266
UhA pp. 430-444

Suggested Written Assignments

1. Discuss the relationship between poetry and music in one of Schubert's songs.
2. Select any five Schubert songs and compare them in these terms: (a) length; (b) key; (c) strophic, varied strophic, or through-composed; (d) degree to which the accompaniment reflects the text.
3. Discuss Schubert's melodic gift as seen in any three of his art songs.
4. Discuss the piano writing in Schubert's art songs.

Footnotes

[1]LpM, p. 780
[2]HaS
[3]CrS, p. 67

chapter 5

the overture: mendelssohn

From the very beginning efforts to evaluate Mendelssohn's position in music history have achieved no general agreement. He is spoken of either with the greatest admiration or in the most derogatory terms, a state of affairs that has come about through the combination of many factors:

1. Mendelssohn's art represents most typically the era of Prussian "Renaissance" under Frederick William IV and this period has not yet been given an unbiased or exhaustive evaluation by historians. It is by no means pure chance that Mendelssohn was sought for service in the King's ambitious plan for Prussia; consequently, something of the same attitude clings to Mendelssohn that was expressed by Prince Metternich, who spoke of Frederick William as a "weak reed in the wind," and "eccentricity . . . in his well-meaning ideas."[1]

2. The phenomenon which allowed the rise of families such as the Mendelssohns into the upper circles of nineteenth-century bourgeois society has never been viewed with real candor by either Jews or Gentiles. Thought in this area is by no means confined to Nazi sentiments, but covers a much larger field of social interaction.

3. The image of a "gentleman of leisure" musician is very difficult to bring into congruence with the customary image of the self-made Romantic composer who had to fight his way across social barriers from very humble origins. In this, Mendelssohn's lively liberal and democratic viewpoints are consistently ignored, even when it can be amply demonstrated that he exercised a great deal more than mere lip service to such ideals.

4. In one sense, Mendelssohn represented a revival of the art of Johann Mattheson (1681-1764) and Georg Philipp Telemann (1681-1767). In an age when harmony might be considered the musical progenitor of melody, Mendelssohn rediscovered the more linear concept of melodic invention associable with the *style galant period.* His melody, more than that of any other composer of the Romantic era, follows the injunctions of the German music encyclopedist, Johann Mattheson, who wrote the definitive work on melodic invention for his period. To a large extent, the "academic" quality of Mendelssohn's music is directly attributable to a revival of writing characteristic of the age of enlightenment, and even Nietzche's description of a "seraphic" quality in his music can be seen as a style of melodic writing strongly reminiscent of François Couperin (1668-1733).

5. Many of his deserving works are not commonly played in contemporary concert halls, tending to give an impression of only certain strengths over others and to discourage their further exploration. Thus the symphonies, the oratorios, the overtures, the concertos, and a certain few select pieces for piano, along with the *Midsummer Night's Dream,* Opus 61, (Overture is Opus 21), music are all well known, but even well-informed musicians know absolutely nothing of his *Lieder* psalms, motets, and chamber music. It is precisely these "known" works that tend to emphasize the Romantic side of his nature; popularity appears to stem from this. The neglected works tend likewise to emphasize the "enlightened" sentiment and "elegant" wit of the eighteenth century; they are "academic," therefore, and are little understood in terms of their own pretensions. It is only when the listener begins to hear both these sides of his musical nature in *all* of his compositions that the versatile and universal composer appears. In terms of today's live performances, this view is simply not possible to gain.

THE OVERTURE OF THE ROMANTIC ERA

During the Romantic era the overture represents a combination of traditional and new elements. The traditional element is its association with the drama which it introduced and from which it derived its dramatic and expressive qualities. Beethoven's overtures were preludes to very specific theater pieces—for his *Fidelio,* Opus 72, H. J. von Collin's *Coriolan,* Opus 62, Goethe's *Egmont,* Opus 84, or the festival plays, *Die Weihe des Hauses,* Opus 124, *König Stephen,* Opus 117, and *Die Ruinen von Athen,* Opus 113. In 1817, Schubert said of his overtures that they were conceived "in the Italian style." Of others, he said that they were written for a comedy, and for some, he said that they were only "incidental music." In 1819 he did not give any explanation at all, and by these successive stages we can observe in one composer the gradual transformation of purpose that was taking place, for the latter compositions were independent instrumental pieces to be performed in their own right as non-theatrical concert literature. In the overtures by Weber, *Der Freischütz* (1821), *Euryanthe* (1823) and *Oberon* (1826), another trend is to be observed, in that these preludes to actual stage works tend to become programmatic pieces very capable of being performed as independent orchestral works. In one sense, they are so complete that they are capable of standing as substitutes for the actual drama itself. The very extreme of this situation appears in the Wagner overtures to *Tannhäuser* (1844), *Lohengrin* (1848) and *Tristan und Isolde* (1859); these are appropriate to the subsequent drama and so shorn of extraneous materials that they give a full orchestral version of the opera before the curtain rises on the sung and acted version. These, too, make excellent programmatic concert material.

Mendelssohn was the first composer to emancipate the overture completely from its theatrical setting. By coining the term *Concert Overture* he quite literally took the overture out of the opera orchestra pit and placed it on the concert stage. In so doing, he rather firmly cut himself off from the programmatic and associative dramatic content formerly borrowed from the stage work, and substituted a much more generalized topical title which had to suffice for all literary or poetic content. The remainder was handled purely by orchestral means, borrowing the sound of operatic expression and the theatrical *tutti.* These he combined with a tightly knit sonata form and introduction thematically linked together in symphonic techniques stemming directly from Beethoven's *Leonore,* Opus 72, B *No. 3,* and *Egmont* overtures. This fusion of the symphonic and operatic emphasized form over expression, the individual sound of instrumental groups over the massed sound of the operatic orchestra, yet retained the essential dramatic approach to thematic development. This new sound of the overture influenced, in turn, the sound of his symphonies, the important overtures all being written between the time of the *First Symphony,* Opus 11, C minor (1824) and the *"Italian" Symphony,* Opus 90, Symphony No. 4, A major-minor (1833):

1826 *Midsummer Night's Dream,* Opus 21
1828 *Meeresstille und Glückliche Fahrt* (Calm Seas and Prosperous Voyage), Opus 27
1830 *Hebrides* (Fingal's Cave), Opus 26
1833 *Das Märchen von der schönen Melusine* (The Fair Melusine), Opus 32

(Other overtures are a youthful "Trumpet Overture" preceding the *Midsummer Night's Dream* and an incidental overture for wind band, Op. 24. Later, in 1843, is the *Ruy Blas,* Opus 95.)

The *Hebrides* overture and the *"Scotch" Symphony,* Opus 56, Symphony No. 3, A minor-major, were both conceived at the same time, and if the symphony is much like an extended overture, (with directions to play the movements without pause), the overture is much like a symphony in one movement. It is from just such single-movement tendencies that the symphonic poems of Franz Liszt were later to be evolved, and out of the amalgamation of opera overture, symphony, and descriptive instrumentation would come the sound of the Strauss tone poem.

MENDELSSOHN'S MELODICISM

Mendelssohn satisfies to a remarkable degree the qualifications for the writing of good melodies as outlined by Johann Mattheson in his *Der Vollkommene Kapellmeister.*[2] Mattheson there states that "the kernel of melodic science" should concentrate upon four qualities: *simplicity, loveliness, precision,* and *linearity.* According to him, the art of making a good melody is positively the most essential element in composition, and that melody furnishes by far the greater portion of the total musical pleasure.

One of the strongest features of Mendelssohn's melody, amounting almost to a trademark, is the use of ascending triadic thrust of the principal subjects of the *String Octet, Op. 20,* the first movement of the *"Italian" Symphony,* and the last movement of the *Violin Concerto,* Op. 64, E minor-major.

Example 1. Mendelssohn, *Octet,* First Movement, Measures 1-4.

The descending triadic figure occurs frequently also; the example from the String Octet, Op. 20, given above illustrates a combination of both ascending and descending triadic formations. The basic motive from the *Hebrides Overture* and the much imitated male-choir setting of *O Täler, weit, o Höhen* furnish excellent examples of the descending triadic motive:

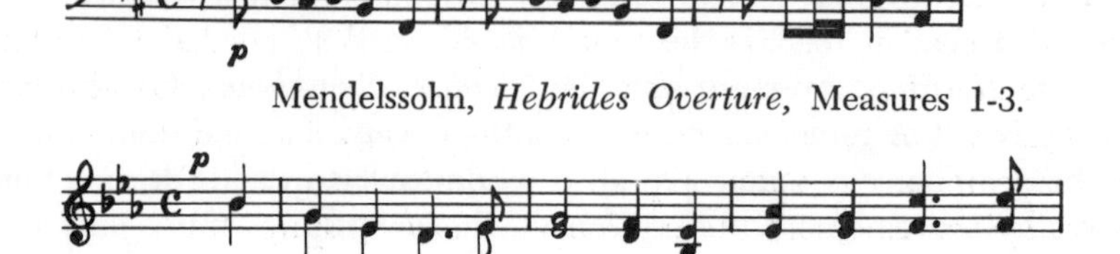

Mendelssohn, *Hebrides Overture,* Measures 1-3.

Example 2. Mendelssohn, *O Täler, weit, o Höhen,* Measures 1-3.

Mattheson's melodic requirements of simplicity, loveliness, precision, and linearity can readily be seen in these examples. Furthermore, a taste for *galant* music can also be traced in Mendelssohn—joyfulness in preference to sadness, pleasurability of music over *Weltschmerz* or "night terrors." The opening measures of the *Midsummer Night's Dream* overture have such a gay, light, and amiable "music of the spirits" air which establishes a definite relationship with the fairy world of Herder and Goethe and which is the very opposite of the sinister view held by Arnim, Brentano, and the brothers Schlegel:

Example 3. Mendelssohn, *A Midsummer Night's Dream Overture,* Measures 8-11.

This melodic outline is very close to a lovely little folk-art song which he composed at the age of eighteen:

Example 4. Mendelssohn, *Maienlied,* Measures 1-4.

THE HEBRIDES OVERTURE

In a letter to Theodore Engelmann, Johannes Brahms wrote, "I would like to give all my works away if I could have succeeded in writing a piece such as the *Hebrides Overture.*" Many other composers also hailed this composition as a masterpiece and as a truly successful combination of classical execution and superbly descriptive music. It was originally entitled "The Lonesome Island," having been inspired by a visit to the Island of Staffa in the Hebrides group off the western coast of Scotland in August of the year 1829. It was not completed until December of 1833. Another composition begun at approximately the same time required an even longer period of incubation; the *"Scotch" Symphony* was not completed until 1842. Although the final title was designated "Hebrides," Mendelssohn did not allow himself to be carried away by the exterior motivation of "sea music." His inspiration was a kind of controlled sentimentality which would make tempestuous sea episodes out of order and completely off balance. Much more in accord with his conception of the *Lieder ohne Worte,* Opuses 19, 30, 38, 53, 62, 67, 85, 102 (Songs without words), he created here a *Lied,* essentially based on a single telling motive, out of which he framed an appealing mood and a classic fabric.

This short melodic formula is an elegant wave motto consisting of the notes of the triad and one passing tone, first in the minor, then in the major. Successive melodic materials are all permutations of the basic motive.

There is a consistent emphasis upon the fifth and third of the chord, the root being clearly enunciated but always abandoned for the dominant note. This allows an ebb and flow of the melodic elaborations to be accompanied by a well-balanced harmonization:

Measures 1 & 2,	I chord
Measures 3 & 4,	III chord
Measures 5 & 6,	V (minor) chord, etc.

This elegant harmonization is colored by an orchestration that takes full advantage of the basic wave motto, patterned alternately in eighth and sixteenth notes. The attentive listener can hear individual instruments or instrument groups, and he will be struck by the fact that Mendelssohn seldom mixes the instrumental families. The first few measures give an excellent insight into Mendelssohn's type of orchestration. In measures 1 to 8, violas, 'cellos, and the first bassoon carry the basic motive in unison, *piano.* The first and second violins sustain an F-sharp for the first six measures, and according to the harmony, this F-sharp is the fifth of the chord in measures 1 and 2, the third of the chord in measures 3 and 4, and the root in measures 5 and 6. The changing function of the F-sharp helps to stress the ebb and flow aspect of the total sound. In the third measure the clarinets add a sustained A—what they have done, of course, is to add the fifth of the new chord (D major). This is sustained through measures 5 and 6, where the oboes add a sustained c-sharp, the fifth of that harmony. Chord roots are given by the string basses, except for the third measure, where the 'cellos break away from the unison to reinforce the new chord with contrary motion. Mendelssohn thus obtains a gradual increase of instrumentation adroitly tied to the harmony and sequential elaboration of the basic wave motive.

Despite a seemingly program-oriented structure, the overture is executed in a remarkably tightly knit sonata movement in which the only irregularity is that of having an abridged recapitulation in favor of an extended *animato* coda. Throughout the whole composition, Mendelssohn preserves the essential "linear" and lyrical melodic line, even in the most animated portions of the development and coda. Arabesques and ornamentations of the "wave" pattern are allowed to be given full development, but they never drown or overwhelm the singing line. At every turn, one is reminded of Mozart by a similarity of craftsmanship, by the buoyant optimism (yet in the minor key), by the elegance of line with its clean harmonic support, and by the ever-present awareness of the relationship between economically realized form and content. By education, temperament, and taste, Mendelssohn showed the hallmarks of a Classical composer, yet, at the same time, he was very much a man of his own times. Romantic currents in his works are reflected in sentimental and passionate qualities and in a continued interest in extramusical, literary, and pictorial references. He lived a very full and active life with many extramusical responsibilities, and it was by dint of concerted hard labor and concentration of effort that he was able to produce a large and meaningful body of works. Never being in want did not seem to have dulled either his perceptions or his ambitions for himself and for the musical profession at large.

Suggested Listening Assignments

1. Mendelssohn, Felix: *Symphony No. 4,* Opus 90 (Italian). How are Mattheson's qualifications for good melodic writing (simplicity, loveliness, precision, linearity) fulfilled in this symphony?
2. Mendelssohn, Felix: *Hebrides Overture,* Opus 26. In what ways is this a programmatic piece of "sea" music? In what ways is it not?

3. WEBER, KARL MARIA VON: *Oberon Overture.* What differences do you notice between this overture and the *Hebrides Overture?* Is Weber's overture as balanced, elegant, and smooth as Mendelssohn's? Do you find concertizing elements in the Weber? In the Mendelssohn?

SUGGESTED ADDITIONAL LISTENING ASSIGNMENTS

1. MENDELSSOHN, FELIX: *Midsummer Night's Dream Music,* Opus 61. What is the relationship between the Overture (Opus 21) and the suite proper? How are the sections related musically to one another?
2. MENDELSSOHN, FELIX: *String Octet,* Opus 20. Listen for the musical form of this composition. What is the function of the various instruments?

SUGGESTED READING ASSIGNMENTS

EaM pp. 124-128
FdA pp. 402-406
GdA pp. 495-499
HaM pp. 828-834
LpM pp. 809-812; 819-820
ScO pp. 275-276
UhA pp. 469-474

SUGGESTED WRITTEN ASSIGNMENTS

1. Study the musical form of Mendelssohn's *Symphony No. 2,* Opus 56. Do you find any "Scotch" elements in this music?
2. To what extent do you find Mendelssohn's music academic? Seraphic?
3. Make a report on Mendelssohn's sacred music.
4. Discuss Mendelssohn's visits to England, his contacts, associations and work while there.

FOOTNOTES

[1]WeM, p. 369
[2]RmJ, p. 138

chapter 6

the opera: weber

THE RISE OF GERMAN NATIONAL OPERA

German composers of opera faced some particularly disheartening conditions in opera at the turn of the nineteenth century. Italian composers still held the key positions as *Kapellmeister* in Vienna, Dresden, and Berlin. Italian opera was enjoying the strongest vogue, and the situation promised to become further stagnated by the fact that tradition still dictated that German composers must go to Italy to study opera composition and production before being acceptable in even minor posts at home. Furthermore, there was a bewildering variety of choices in genre available to the composer, all of which posed very special challenges and opportunistic possibilities: the Italian *opera seria, semi-seria, opera buffa,* the French *opéra comique* and revolutionary opera, and the many types of German *Singspiele.* In addition, there was the formidable example of Mozart's *Figaro* K. 492 and *Don Giovanni* K. 527 which were steadily gaining in popularity, pointing the way toward further cross-breeding and development of genres.

Essentially the most pressing problems facing German composers revolved around the fact that there was no German equivalent of a Paris to centralize German opera activity. A vital German National Theater had been established in Mannheim-Darmstadt at the very end of the eighteenth century, but it had unfortunately not generated an opera tradition in its wake, and it is highly significant that neither Weber nor Meyerbeer found any nationalistic stimuation there during apprenticeship years under Abbé Vogler. In Vienna, the *Singspiel* seemed unable to grow out of its level of comfortable provincialism, and it became fixed in a "Biedermeier" style typified by the composers Joseph Weigl (1766-1846) and Adalbert Gyrowetz (1763-1850). In Berlin, a potentially vital form consisting of suitelike successions of folk tunes and composed popular songs called the *Liederspiel* was given an initial impetus by Johann Reichardt and was picked up by Mendelssohn and Gustav Albert Lortzing (1801-1851), but their efforts led only to stagnation on a type of variety show called the *Berliner Posse.*

Meanwhile, Romanticism had been, in certain very notable cases, quietly invading the German opera by way of the libretti. Beethoven's long search for a suitable libretto had resolved itself in *Fidelio,* the story of which embodied current French democratic ideals and focused upon a future all-consuming theme of woman as rescuer-redemptor. Mozart's *Don Giovanni* recast the Classic stock character of Don Juan inside a magic circle cast by the ponderously supernatural "Stone Guest," and in *Die Zauberflöte,* Mozart and Schikaneder created a veritable pastiche of Romantic elements reaching all the way from Masonic overtones to the world of magical fantasy.

WEBER

The stage was set for *Der Freischütz.* Karl Maria von Weber grew up in a thoroughly Romantic atmosphere. His father was a restless and roving adventurer, soldier, theatrical director, and municipal musician, and his mother had died prematurely exhausted by the rigors of childbearing and such uncongenial nomadic life. Weber's earliest training was with Michael Haydn (1737-1806) in Salzburg. Later, he studied with the highly controversial Abbé (Georg Joseph) Vogler (1749-1814), who procured for him the position as conductor in the Breslau opera house. Soon thereafter, his reputation as conductor and piano virtuoso rather well-established, he began a period of nomadic barnstorming which took him all over Europe. Appointment as conductor of the Prague Opera in 1813 resulted in a very stormy but highly successful three-year tenure, and he moved to a similar post in Dresden, where he remained until his death at the age of forty. A large portion of his best instrumental operas, *Der Freischütz, Euryanthe,* and *Oberon* were all written during the Dresden tenure. Of these, *Der Freischütz* is his greatest masterpiece.

DER FREISCHÜTZ

The *Waldhorn* (forest horn) sounds the first notes of *Der Freischütz,* symbolically proclaiming the primacy of the forest in the drama. All of the characters in the play are deeply imbued with the encompassing forest. Not only is it their livelihood, but the source of their spiritual life as well, for it represents the forces of nature which surround man at all times. Thus, the forest can be ominous, threatening, and horrible, as it is in the "Wolf's Glen," and in such circumstances, the destinies of its inhabitants are all but determined. Max, the assistant ranger, escapes the power of invisible forces, however, through the agency of faith and moral strength. The *Freischütz* libretto epitomizes the Romantic literature of the times. Its people are the simple country folk who live close to nature and share in a sense of unity of life with nature. Its setting is also a land of escape, and identification with the anonymous folktale, and a sharing of wonderment at the miraculous, supernatural powers at work in the affairs of men. Its horrible and extravagant elements dramatize the dark side of real life, but by their very extremes lighten the human role. And its beauties, like the beauties of the forest, serve as an agency of transcendence into a true identity of life with nature.

In its musical forms, *Der Freischütz* makes some decisive departures from operatic traditions. Mozart's operas, even those like *Die Zauberflöte* that introduce Romantic elements, adhere to the *da capo* aria, the *Lied,* and the ensemble finale without ever hinting that freedom from the closed forms was either demanded or desirable. Weber had the least success when he followed the closed forms, as is evidenced by Caspar's traditional vengeance aria in Italian *opera seria* style, "Der Hölle Netz hat dich umgarnt" (Act I, No. 5, p. 53). Such an aria is no match for the unorthodox "Hier im irdschen Jammerthal," also sung by Caspar (Act I No. 4, p. 48), where accentuation at the final cadence is on the dominant otherwise traditional bridal march song, "Wir winden dir den Jungfernkranz" (Act III, No. 14, p. 126), and the recurrent A-flat played by the violas in the instrumental postlude create an ominous note of foreboding and anticipation of coming events. The country waltz (Act I, No. 3, p. 38) is broken up into small *poco a poco morendo* fragments, anticipating the text of the recitative by Max which follows, "Nein! länger trag ich nicht die Qualen, die Angst, die jede Hoffnung raubt" (No! I can bear my fate no longer. All hope is banished from my soul). The same waltz also precedes an aria the text of which has to do with forests, meadows, and the happy life Max experienced while living there.

The overture to *Der Freischütz* is most remarkable because of its merger of the sonata-allegro form and of purely operatic materials dealing with nature. In the "Wolf's Glen" scene, Weber presents a series of images juxtaposed with intentional unrelatedness, creating a kaleidoscopic effect. A similar type of image series also appears in the *Oberon* overture, and it is perhaps significant that the kaleidoscope was invented in the same years that Weber was laboring on these works.[1] Some orchestrations are also developed in a kaleidoscopic manner by the singling out of isolated special colors of solo instruments. In the *Freischütz* overture the clarinet is given a prominent solo high above tremolo strings, and later the lowest registers of the clarinet are mixed with *pizzicati* basses to produce a very dark color. Another passage in the development breaks up the traditional three-part formation of trombones into an echo motive all their own.

More than any other factor, it was the incorporation of folk elements that dictated Weber's departures from the traditional closed forms. Using a musical language close to the German folk song and folk dance necessitated elimination of many factors which typified Italian and French formalized styles. The German middle-class audience, now an emancipating artistic force, recognized immediately the full import of music as a national expression, and they took *Der Freischütz* to their hearts. Thus in making himself the friend of the great middle-class audience, Weber tapped a strong vein of nationalism that had been long dormant or suppressed in German musical life. Even today it is *Der Freischütz* that is the German opera *par excellence,* and not the more self-conscious *Die Meistersinger* (1867) by Wagner.

Suggested Listening Assignments

1. Weber, Karl Maria von: *Der Freischütz, Finale of Act II*: *"Wolf-Glen Scene."* By what musical means does Weber obtain his dramatic effects? How does he handle the orchestra? What other sound effects are present?
2. Weber, Karl Maria von: *Der Freischütz.* What is the style of the choral numbers of this opera? Are they complex? Folk song-like?
3. Weber, Karl Maria von: *Der Freischütz.* Listen for the "unorthodox" arias as explained in this chapter (Act I, No. 4; Act III, No. 14, Act I, No. 3).

Suggested Additional Listening Assignments

1. Weber, Karl Maria von: *Euryanthe.* Listen for the through-composed patterns in the vocal solo numbers of this opera.
2. Weber, Karl Maria von: *Oberon Overture.* What is the Romantic element in Weber's orchestration of this music?
3. Weber, Karl Maria von: *Der Freischütz.* Listen to the country dance in this opera. Compare it to Weber's *Invitation to the Dance.* What do both pieces have in common? What is different?

Suggested Reading Assignments

Cbt pp. 364-368
EaM pp. 104-116
FdA pp. 460-466
GdA pp. 558-561
HaM pp. 736-740
LpM pp. 793-800
ScO pp. 261-263
UhA pp. 428-430; 449-451

part III

MUSIC, LITERATURE, AND THE ARTS

chapter 7

the poetic imagination: schumann

SCHUMANN, MUSIC CRITIC

Schumann's first critical essay dealt with the *Don Juan Variations,* Op. 2, of Chopin, in 1831 and real German music criticism may be said to originate with that essay. Schumann was intensely interested in constructive criticism and in discovery of the outstanding talents of his own times, openly championing Chopin, Berlioz, Mendelssohn, and Brahms. From the very first, Schumann's writings were distinguished by their enthusiasm and singular imagination approach. They were cast in the form of dialogues between imaginary characters, the romantically turbulent Florestan, the thoughtful and sensitive Eusebius, and Master Raro, a synthesis of the two (Cla*RA RO*bert; his wife and himself), all of which was patterned after Hoffman's *Die Serapionsbrüder* and Jean Paul's *Flegeljahre* and *Siebenkäs.*

PIANO MUSIC

Schumann was master of the short, self-contained "character piece" for the piano. These often formed a cycle, such as the *Papillons,* Op. 2, *Carneval,* Op. 9, *Kreisleriana,* Op. 16, *Waldszenen,* Op. 82, and *Kinderszenen,* Op. 15. Frequently, titles indicated a general poetic idea behind the whole cycle, as in *Carneval* and *Papillons;* in other instances, they were collective titles, as in *Waldszenen* and *Kinderszenen,* with specific subtitles referring to a number of single scenes from the forest or the Romantic world of childhood. Musical unity in such a cycle has been achieved by maintaining subtle relationships among the various movements. An excellent example is the *Kinderszenen,* a composition often mistakenly identified as a suite of completely independent pieces, but which is very definitely constructed on the principle of thematic metamorphosis. Each movement of the cycle recasts the core theme to illustrate a slightly different facet of the general poetic theme.

Evidence of a great admiration for the polyphony of J. S. Bach continually shows through the textures of Schumann's piano pieces. These generally come in the inner voices, sometimes in strongly individual bass lines; almost never are the accompanying voices formed in static harmonic blocks. Here or there will be a trace of independence, sometimes even a bit of the quixotic, but it will always be suitable to the poetry of the moment. The result is that the same "Wonderful weaving-together" of melodies (wunderbare Verflechtung) which Schumann so admired in Bach can be seen in the works of the disciple.

Example 1. Schumann, *Albumblätter,* Op. 124, No. 5, Measures 1-4.

VOCAL MUSIC

It was only after he had written the majority of his compositions for the piano (Op. 1 to Op. 23) that Schumann discovered his affinity for the art song. That was 1840, and in that same year he composed 138 songs—more than half of his entire output in this category. Poetry for his songs was drawn from Heine (Cycle, Op. 24 and *Dichterliebe,* Op. 48), Kerner (Cycle, Op. 35), Chamisso (*Frauenliebe und Leben,* Op. 42), Rückert (*Liebesfrühling,* Op. 37), Eichendorff (Cycle, Op. 39), and passages from Goethe and Byron. His choices identify him completely with the great "*Weltschmerz*" poetry of his own time, poetry which dealt with tender sentiments with nearly pathological condition of the suffering lover. Songs such as "Wenn ich in deine Augen seh," Op. 48, No. 4, and "Aus meinen Tränen spriessen," Op. 48, No. 2, achieve the finest expression of these emotions.

Schumann came to the art song by way of the piano; his accompaniments therefore play a most important role in the song. The melodic lyricism which Schumann had cultivated in his piano compositions spilled over into his production of songs, where it served a double purpose. In the art song, Schumann could weave a strong polyphonic texture of interacting voice and instrument, projecting still further the poetic elements already present in his piano compositions.

Romantic strivings are evident in many ways in Schumann's songs. Simple folklike qualities are achieved in songs such as "Volksliedchen," Op. 51, No. 2, "Marienwürmchen," Op. 79, No. 13, "Sonnenschein," Op. 36, No. 4, "Die Soldatenbraut," his "Sonntags am Rhein," Op. 36, No. 1, and others, representing not only a Rousseau-like return to nature, but a definite attempt to elevate expression to the universal and transcendent. Here economy of means signifies a deepening of expression, with diatonic melodies and simple harmonies in a predominant role. Chromaticism, when resorted to, is used with caution, and enharmonic effects are reserved to depicting only the most unusual of circumstances—the supernatural, for example. Another Romantic element, the cultivation of melancholy, is also present in Schumann's songs. Almost all of them are permeated with a wistful aura of gentle sadness and spiritual *malaise* that is at once childlike in its spontaniety and highly sophisticated in its systematic cultivation.

SCHUMANN'S SCENES FROM FAUST

It seemed inevitable that every Romantic should make an attempt to interpret *Faust* (1853), and Schumann was no exception. It is interesting to note that Schumann cast his version in the form of an oratorio-like work which called for vocal writing quite different from his art songs. The aspect of the Faust story that attracted Schumann most strongly was the figure of the protagonist as restless searcher for truth and beauty, a figure which Schumann portrays as a projection of his own Florestan-Eusebius dichotomy. For this, Schumann cast Faust in a dramatic baritone part, the music of which was much closer to Wagner's continuously-evolving vocal line (of *Der Fliegende Holländer* (1841) and Tannhäuser) than to his accustomed style. Gretchen's aria before the picture of the *Mater Dolorosa* is perhaps one of the most perfect songs Schumann ever wrote, and in the finale of the third section, his inspiration remains at a consistently high level. The concluding *Chorus*

Mysticus is an extended double chorus beginning with a splendid "hermetic" canon on the words, "All things corruptible are but a parable." This chorus leads to the final jubilation, "Eternal womanhood leads us on high," maintaining the mystical tone of the poetry into a final ethereal *decrescendo*. At the words "Here it is done" a motiv is stated which is the second subject of the *allegro* section of the overture. It functions as a leading motto, or as a motive of reminiscence since it appears prominently at the beginning of Nos. 3, 5, and 8.

THE SYMPHONIES

The same Florestan-Eusebius dichotomy which Schumann felt in his own personality exists in the symphonic works in a most striking form. Here the forces of opposition are on the one hand formal classical discipline and on the other a highly intuitive element which has been stronger and determined the very nature of each composition.

One specific device that lends much charm and poetic quality to the symphonies is the introduction of the before-mentioned leading motto, at certain key points. These mottos—not to be confused with the Wagnerian *Leitmotiv*—are generally drawn from the Introduction of the first movement. Their repetition at later points gives a certain amount of organic unity of mood and thematic material to the entire symphony. In the *First Symphony*, Op. 38 ("Spring"), B-flat major, a motto appears at the beginning of the recapitulation and of the coda of the *Allegro* movement; in the *Fourth Symphony*, Op. 120, d minor, the main section of the introduction reappears as a frame of the *Romanza* movement, and it also plays an important role in the shaping of the first subject of the *Allegro movement*. In addition to the use of the leading motto, there are also some instances of musical transplantations from movement to movement. In the *Fourth Symphony*, the middle part of the *Romanza* is used again as the trio of the scherzo, and the headmotive of the first movement is used in the transition between scherzo and finale. Such devices are, of course, nothing but an extension of the musical epigram, so skillfully developed in his piano works. This epigrammatic technique, epitomized by the short introduction to *Papillons* or the themes of the *Abegg Variations*, Op. 1, may also be observed in his prose writing (as, for instance, in *On Music and Musicians*) as well as in the symphonies. He overcame the essential terseness of this epigrammatic style by borrowing materials from their traditional formal places and by ingeniously weaving them together into other movements, thus achieving a feeling of organic growth. It is in this facility of weaving together motives that would otherwise be static in nature or stanzaic in traditional treatments that Schumann displays some of his most vital symphonic writing. A natural result of this "woven" texture is that various movements of symphonies are joined together without pause. The *Fourth Symphony,* for instance, was at first called a symphonic fantasia since all movements are joined by clever harmonic couplings or transitional passages. Another device is the insertion of an extra movement between the third movement and the finale of the "Rhenish" Symphony, Op. 97, E-flat major—a vaguely programmatic mood piece which was at first inscribed, "in the manner of a solemn ceremony."

The intimacy of the Romantic poetic symphony is well portrayed in the slow movements of the symphonies. Although the slow movement of the *First Symphony* is a *Larghetto,* that of the *Third* a *Moderato,* and that of the *Fourth* a *Romanza,* all approach the symphonic intermezzo with song-like elements, later to become very prominent in the symphonies of Brahms.

One of the greatest departures from the Classical norm appears in the first movement of the *Fourth Symphony.* It has no recapitulation; instead, there is a lengthy development containing a second subject not introduced in the exposition. Most of the development is repeated in transposition in the manner of literary repetition of extended sentences. Following this, there is an extended coda. Such an irregularity could not have been the product of mere Romantic instability, for Schumann's goals were the Classical forms and Beethoven his ideal. Strong programmatic promptings must have dictated these deviations. In his essays Schumann readily admitted, both by implication and by explicit wording, that literary programs, poetic images, and impressions of nature played a large role in the fashioning of the majority of his piano works, most of which already bore rather definite explanatory titles. However, he was far more reticent about disclosing titles and underlying programs for his symphonies, and even went so far as to suppress titles originally attached to the movements of the B-flat symphony and two movements of the E-flat Symphony. No doubt he feared that an admission of programmatic origin might serve to detract from their value as abstract music, for he had stated in an essay on Berlioz that "if the eye is once directed to a certain point, the ear can no longer judge independently." Yet, for all his circumspection, the programmatic nature of his symphonies is easily apparent, and it is this infusion of extra-musical associations that reserves a special place for Schumann in the hierarchy of the Romantic symphony writers. He opened up a new world of Romantic imagery, a very personal kind of utterance which sprang from the same roots as his beloved Jean Paul Richter.

Suggested Listening Assignments

1. Schumann, Robert: *Papillons,* Opus 2. Can you hear how the composer achieves unity in this cycle through motivic repetitions or variations? Through the same atmosphere in all the pieces?
2. Schumann, Robert: *Aus meinen Tränen spriessen,* Opus 48, No. 2. How does the composer achieve the feeling of "tediousness of the world" through music? Is the vocal lyricism the outgrowth of the piano part?
3. Schumann, Robert: *Symphony No. 4,* Opus 120. Can you make out the leading motto? How are other materials transplanted from one movement to the next? Can you hear the irregular sonata allegro treatment of the first movement?

Suggested Additional Listening Assignments

1. Schumann, Robert: The slow movements of his four symphonies. Are these similar in expression? Are they like the composer's slow piano pieces?
2. Schumann, Robert: *Symphony in E-Flat Major,* Opus 97. How does Schumann handle the variation technique here? What is the Germanic quality of this music? Do you hear any polyphonic techniques used?

Suggested Reading Assignments

CbT pp. 356-358
EaM pp. 205-209; 128-132; 186-189
FdA pp. 406-415
GdA pp. 515-516; 534-535
HaM pp. 817-828
LpM pp. 812-814; 819-825
CcO pp. 282-284
UhA pp. 474-480

Suggested Written Assignments

1. Compare Schumann's handling of the DIES IRAE in his *Scenes from Faust* with Berlioz' treatment of the DIES IRAE in his *Requiem.*
2. Describe Schumann's genius as a master of the epigram in any one of his piano cycles.
3. Discuss the importance of the introduction (thematic reservoir) of Schumann's *Fourth Symphony* in relation to the entire work.
4. Select a song by Schumann and one by Schubert. Compare them in every way you can: source of text, subject, length, accompaniment, mood, etc.
5. Write about the importance of Clara Schumann in the life of her husband.

Footnotes

[1]MdS

chapter 8

the idée fixe: berlioz

THE IMAGE OF BERLIOZ

Romain Rolland, speaking of Berlioz, saw in him a "sense for pure beauty" of a very French classical nature, and cited the entrance of Andromache in *The Trojans* (1859) as an example of "antique sublimity" that linked Berlioz with Christoph Willibald Gluck (1714-1787) and Racine.[1] This is by far not the usual view, but Berlioz even today remains, as he always was, a most controversial figure in music. He had, to be sure, a strong vein of admiration for Vergil which had been instilled in him by his physcian-scientist father, and *The Trojans* is only one of many references to antiquity in his works.

The more usual image of Berlioz is drawn in large part from his *Mémoirs* and from the supposedly autobiographical program of the *Symphonie Fantastique*, Op. 14, which cast him in Byronesque postures bound to be misleading.[2] The literary style of these sources is based upon that of Victor Hugo's *Hernani* which was performed in Paris February 25, 1830, while the *Symphonie Fantastique* was given only a few months later, December 5, 1830. Young Berlioz absorbed the style and the Romantic ideals of Hugo just as quickly as he absorbed his musical training—a process that took place so fast that many still tend to think of him as untrained. Also in Paris at the same time was an English company playing Shakespeare, and Berlioz fell in love with the leading lady, Harriet Smithson. He pursued this love with the same intensity as his pursuit of musical ideals, and with the same lack of realism. Years later they were married, but reality could not keep that flame alive. Likewise, any first performance of his works seemed bound to be a *succès d'estime,* but there was never any number of performances to cover the concert debts.

A sophisticated segment of the newly expanded nineteenth-century audience took a genuine interest in music which was new and different. Therefore, many concerts were devoted to performances of new works, and here Berlioz was well received. He was also highly respected as a music journalist and counted upon this vocation for most of his earnings. At the same time there was a second type of audience which asserted itself very strongly. This group distinguished itself by its lack of comprehension of quality and nuance. Once a composer was acclaimed by the majority of these people, audience responses conformed to their reactions. Composers like Henri Herz (1803-1888) and Sigismond Thalberg (1812-1871) thrived under these conditions, and in their works aimed at the cultural mentality of the "average" listener. They were revered as the greatest composers of the age, while Berlioz was considered a slightly ludicrous figure because his genuine inventiveness would never allow him to repeat the popular clichés. He was greatly embittered by this lack of support when he published the famous *Traité d'instrumentation* (1844), a work still consulted today.

THE "ISOLATION OF MAN" THEME

The Romantic theme of the "Isolation of Man," appears in Berlioz's works—*The Corsaire,* Op. 21, *Lélio,* Op. 14, *Harold in Italy,* Op. 16, and *Damnation of Faust,* Op. 24. This theme portrays man as surrounded by a hostile world, and this individual is seen as emerging alone and incomplete. Perhaps this was due to the ever-increasing division of labor and to the spread of specialization which resulted in the "I" opposed to the immense mass who must face society alone as a stranger among strangers.

Berlioz lived to see all his loved ones die: father, mother, wife, mistress, and only son. Repeated blows of fate, continual financial uncertainty, and the extremes to which his own volatile nature drove him, combined to make his life the prototype of the Romantic artist's role. Ironically, this Romantic had dreamed of a much different *dénouement.* The incongruence of ideal and reality seemed only to spur his imagination. He produced works generally judged to be his best, the *Damnation of Faust,* Op. 24, *The Trojans* (1859), and *The Childhood of Christ,* Op. 25, in circumstances continually aggravated by illness, discouragement, and feelings of unfulfilled promise and unrealized goals.

MELODY

Berlioz followed the Mannheim and Vienna traditions very closely, and in many respects the simple machinery of his scores appears to come straight from Beethoven and Schubert models. In that context, however, the harmonies are gauche, if not wrong—a quality which Berlioz's critics have been quick to label as amateurish. Viewed in the light of what he was attempting to do, they are bold and daring and capable of achieving remarkable variety with surprisingly economical means. Berlioz pioneered the asymmetrical balance of phrase. The second half of a melodic period, for instance, frequently has small variants, extensions, and alterations, all of which can be seen as amplifications of the techniques of the last period quartets of Beethoven—music that had horrified the Parisians even as late as 1850. Actually Berlioz's melodies are extremely varied and expressive. They exhibit the felicity of Italian vocalism, the sententiousness of the German *Lied*, and frequently also the charm of the French folk song. His pliant flowing recitatives with phrases of unusual lengths (up to twenty measures) are particularly notable. It is obvious that the composer had carefully studied French models in Lully, Jean-Philippe Rameau (1683-1764), and Christoph Willibald Gluck, (1714-1787) and had profited enormously by their examples.

SACRED MUSIC

The colossal and monumental elements of Berlioz's works, shown in the *Te Deum*, Op. 22, for orchestra, organ, and three choirs, or the *Requiem*, Op. 5, for massive orchestra, chorus, soloists, and "four orchestras of brass instruments placed 'round the main orchestra and the mass of voices," trace their genesis back to Beethoven and an English tradition of choral music with orchestra. Both Classic and Romantic composers had been stimulated by the continued success of Handel's *Messiah*, and had turned away from composition for the church service itself. In the concert hall they could indulge in liturgical freedoms and in the greater variety afforded by the larger forces available. The social implications of this shift of public expression of religion from the church to the concert hall were far-reaching. Mainly, it was demonstrated that democratic institutions outside the church could operate as centers of religious, artistic, and social importance as well as political centers. It is highly significant that a public performance, supported entirely by single paid admissions and attended by a wide segment of society, should thus become endowed with so many cultural attributes. The whole that had been partitioned, in previous eras, among numerous small court spheres and a reformation-divided church was now finding a totality of expression not only in the market places but in social meeting halls. The immediate models for Berlioz were massive compositions at patriotic festivals during the French Revolution. They were written by composers such as François Gossec (1734-1829), Etienne Méhul (1763-1817), and Rodolphe Kreutzer (1766-1831). They were scores for large masses and Berlioz likewise set out to realize in a most concrete way an ideal of composition for truly large musical forces.

THE SYMPHONIE FANTASTIQUE

Beethoven's *"Pastoral" Symphony,* Op. 68, F major, is usually named as the prototype for the programmatic symphony, but almost any of Beethoven's nine symphonies, particularly the third and ninth, in which the element of dramatic conflict plays a large role, might just as well be named the predecessor of Berlioz's symphonies. In the case of Beethoven the music is a revelation of a very strong personality seeking self-realization by indentification with heroic figures (No. 3), renewal in nature (No. 6), or brotherhood (No. 9). These are all expressed in terms that reflect inner tensions, conflicts, and resolution. Their nature precludes the necessity of a program, and they still operate within the framework of abstraction. Berlioz's dramatic symphonies operate on a considerably more externalized basis. An important clue to the nature of this difference is found in the preface to Victor Hugo's *Cromwell,* where the dramatist calls for a "new dramatic reality" which "originates from the union of two types, the sublime and the grotesque." Berlioz's execution of this kind of opposition assigned separate movements of his *Symphonie Fantastique* to disparate imaginary moods; i.e. "Walpurgis' Night," and "March to the Scaffold." These differ from Beethoven in that they represent experiences *imagined* and *external* to the composer, and although these experiences are very sympathetically portrayed and transmitted through the composer, they do not have the consistency of Beethoven's strength of character to draw them together into a unit. It is very significant that when the time came for Berlioz to assign a program to the *Fantastique,* he set it in terms of a distraught artist in various states of delusions. Such a cast of characters, consisting of but one person (plus delusions), tended to draw and work back to the Beethovian orbit; unfortunately, audiences very logically construed it as autobiographical.

THE IDÉE FIXE

The Symphonie Fantastique has an introduction very much resembling Beethoven's Sonata Pathétique, especially in the use of dotted rhythms and the appoggiatura. The famous *Idée fixe* handles the rising sixth in a Beethoven-like way, except that it has one pedal point chord as accompaniment.

This famous melody was first used in a work which gained for Berlioz the second prize at the *Prix de Rome* Competition. In that setting, it accompanied the heroine, Herminie, a female warrior, so it is clear that it was not irrevocably linked with Hariett Smithson. When Berlioz identified it as such (Letter of April 16, 1849), ten years after the production of the *Symphonie Fantastique,* the marriage had about run its course, and he may have wanted to strike a pose in the manner of Chateaubriand's *René,* the French Romantic equivalent of Goethe's *Werther.* No such identifications occurred during the actual writing of the symphony. Most likely, Berlioz was quick to perceive a very fundamental flaw in the "new reality" approach to the symphonic drama—the more successful he was in portraying the various dream states, each occupying a separate symphonic movement, the more disparate and unrelated they would become. So, in order to unify a dangerously splintered work, he resorted to the recurrent theme of the *idée fixe.* In actuality, he did not need to resort to such a mechanical means, for the dramaturgy of sequence and timing furnished a unity that would have been sufficient in itself as an organic development.

THE COLORISTIC ORCHESTRA

One of the striking new features of the *Symphonie Fantastique* was its conception of the coloristic orchestra. Berlioz conceived his thematic materials in terms of individual instrumental sounds, and even early sketches of his works have the instrumentation carefully indicated. For him, sound and timbre assumed the utmost importance, and it seemed almost as if, in his mind, each instrument possessed a highly charged force. His thematic invention is closely bound up with coloristic combinations especially adapted to the expression of the grotesque, the grandiose, and the romantically nostalgic. In this sense, he continued a tradition of French musicians who exhibited, along with the creative faculty, theoretical excellence. In the eighteenth century, for instance, Rameau had formulated a complete theory of musical expression complementary to his new theory of chordal structure. Similarly, by example and by his *Traité d'instrumentation,* Berlioz laid the foundation for an entirely new esthetic based upon the expressive possibilities of the various timbres of the orchestra. An idea of the importance of this instrumental usage can be gained from following the *idée fixe* through the first movement of the *Symphonie Fantastique.* Its first presentation in the introduction (measures 71-86) is without accompaniment. In its next appearance, as pseudo-second subject (measures 150-157), the flute is doubled by violins and violas and further enriched by additional accompaniment figures in the second violins and cellos. It is given another statement in the *dolce* combination of flute, oboe, and clarinet, against an accompaniment of strings (measures 238-278), with still more instruments added in the course of its extension. After being played by full orchestra (measures 410-439), it is broken up into an imitative play of short statements by flute, oboe, clarinet, and bassoon (measures 451-461).

Of Berlioz's later works, only *Harold in Italy* retained the one-person cast of characters. Here again he used the cyclic motive, unifying the movements with a technique similar to that of the *idée fixe.* The other dramatic symphonies call for a much larger cast, with the result that the possibility of imputed autobiographical content was much reduced. Larger canvases also opened new possibilities for the reworking of traditional forms to meet the conditions of "new reality," particularly in the expression of conflicts between the real and the ideal.

After *Harold,* Berlioz turned to grander projects, utilizing voices as well as the orchestra. He approached, if not exceeded, the dimensions of Wagner's *Ring* with *The Trojans,* which he described as a *tragédie lyrique* and for which he, like Wagner, wrote his own libretto. This point was reached by way of *Romeo and Juliet,* Opus 17 (grand dramatic symphony) and *Damnation of Faust* (*opéra de concert*). His last work for the theater, *Beatrice and Benedict* (1862), is smaller in dimensions (two acts) and lighter in subject.

Suggested Listening Assignments

1. Berlioz, Hector: *Symphony Fantastique,* Opus 14. What is the melodic quality of the *idée fixe*? Can you trace it throughout the entire work?
2. Berlioz, Hector: *Requiem,* Opus 5. Can you hear any similarity between the sound of Handel's *Messiah* and the sound of the *Requiem*? How is the orchestration handled in the *tuba mirum* part of the *Dies irae*?
3. Berlioz, Hector: *Harold in Italy.* In what ways does Berlioz write programmatic music in this work? How is it connected with Bryon's poem? How is the cyclic motive treated in this work?

Suggested Additional Listening Assignments

1. Berlioz, Harold: *The Trojans.* What musical treatment does Cassandra, the protagonist of the drama, receive? What kind of music do you hear in the great visionary arias of the first act? How does her music project the tragic power of FATE which pervades the entire work?
2. Berlioz, Harold: *Childhood of Christ,* Opus 25. Listen for specific effects: (a) the bolero-like orchestration (Ravel) in the *Marche Nocturne;* (b) the choir of angels in the 6th scene of Act I; (c) the exquisite overture at the beginning of the second part.

Suggested Reading Assignments

CbT pp. 368-372
EaM pp. 132-140
FdA pp. 428-434
GdA pp. 535-538
HaM pp. 759-781
LpM pp. 859-864
ScO pp. 278-280
UhA pp. 490-493

Suggested Written Assignments

1. Discuss the importance of Romantic elements in Berlioz's music with respect to (a) harmonic materials; (b) orchestral innovations; (c) choice of texts; (d) handling of Classical forms; (e) relationship to the heritage of Beethoven's music.
2. Read some of Berlioz's *Evenings in an Orchestra*. Give a report on his personality as you would judge it from this book.
3. Discuss Berlioz and the French audiences.

Footnotes

[1]SwB, p. 237
[2]EeB, p. 525

chapter 9

the symphonic poem: liszt

In order to fully understand the program music of this era, one must become aware of two very distinct aspects of its fundamental nature: the quality of *descriptive* and the quality of *poetic* music. The descriptive qualities are exactly what the name implies—the pictorial and representational in music. However, the concept of poetic music will need considerable elaboration.

MENDELSSOHN'S SONGS WITHOUT WORDS (LIEDER OHNE WORTE)

It appears that the name, *Song Without Words,* was first coined by Felix Mendelssohn in collaboration with his sister Fanny in 1822, but examples of that type of composition can be found as early as half a century before. In the preface of a song collection made by Johann Wilhelm Hertel (1727-1789) in 1760, we find the very interesting comment:

> ". . . One need not always sing these songs aloud, but sometimes one can play them on the *Clavier* while one imagines the words and the passions of the text in one's mind only. . . ."[1]

Certainly the spirit of this little preface catches the essence of Mendelssohn's intriguing use of the title, *Song Without Words.* By its own subtle suggestion, the title challenges the listener to ask exactly what the content of the missing words might be. There is an open invitation for the listener to indulge in whatever flight of fancy may fit his mood of the moment.

There are precursors to Mendelssohn's compositions. Wilhelm Taubert (1811-1891) wrote some *Minnelieder for the Pianoforte* which bore an abbreviated motto at the beginning of the composition conveying lyrics for the ensuing music. The poems were not necessarily intended to be sung to the music, but the song is very definitely recognizable in the melody of the piano part.[2] Later editions of these works were entitled *Songs Without Words.* Other examples which Mendelssohn must have known about were Johann Wenzel Tomaschek's (1774-1850)*Eklogues* (1807), *Rhapsodies* (1810) and *Dittirambi* (1818).

PROGRAM MUSIC WITH TEXT MOTTOS

Using the basic principle of Taubert's *Minnelieder for the Pianoforte,* Liszt composed a number of piano works entitled *Liebesträume, Nottornos, Sonnettos, Etudes* and *Harmonies Poétiques et Religieuses.* In each case, a text is placed immediately under the title. The celebrated *Liebestraum No. 3* has four stanzas of a poem by Freiligrath taken from a collection called *Zwischen den Garben* (1849), the poems of which in general imitate the literary style of Victor Hugo. When one compares the first two stanzas of the poem with the melody of the *Liebestraum,* one finds that it fits very neatly into the first section of the composition (key of A-flat major, up to the first cadenza), and that it could be sung in the manner of an art song with the same accompanimental piano part. Likewise, the third stanza fits the following section (in B major), and the fourth stanza fits the ensuing section (in C major). In the original poem, the fifth stanza is a repeat of the first, and it therefore fits the *da capo* ending (in A-flat major). It is quite apparent that Liszt intended the words to dramatize the context of the music in a very literal sense, not to be sung, perhaps, but to be imagined or read while listening.

The musical form of all these *Liebesträume-Nottornos* is that of the theme and variations, adapted to the pattern of a strophic song. Dramatic changes of key, climaxed by cadenza passages, serve to separate the successive stanzas of the poem and to heighten the effect. To this series of strophes, Liszt added his versatile inventory of accompanimental variations—chordal figurations in sixths and tenths, crossed-hands leaps, chromaticisms, and garlands of secondary seventh-chords—over which the dominating melody and its complimentary rich bass line soar with empyrean grace. The mixture of genres is very skillful: Basically, they are character pieces of compositions which exploit a single theme of simple nature or a set of two contrasting themes. To this underlying structural idea he added the concept of the *Song Without Words,* even supplying complete texts, relating the genre with the strophic song. In addition, he added the subtitle *Nocturne,* suggesting a subtle connection with another Romantic tradition, that of the night-piece, a form that had become extremely popular in both poetry and music in response to the cult of the night, with its moonlit charms and terrors. The matrix of the *Nocturne* was furnished by Chopin and John Field (1782-1837), who cast it in a three part song form consisting of an elegaic "A" section followed by a strongly contrasted, frequently very agitated "B" section, with a return to the elegiac "A" section. Liszt observed the spirit of this form by confining the more dramatic variations of his "strophes" to the middle section, but on the whole, his versions operate upon a much higher and volatile plane of tension.

Liszt wrote three compositions interpreting the sonnets of Petrarch. Sonnets numbers 47, 104, and 123 could be sung in the same manner as the *Liebesträume*. Likewise, his *Pensée de Minuit* and *Méditation d'après poésie de Lamartine* are designed to go with specific texts. All of these compositions have a close correlation with their preceding motto-texts, both in mood and lyrical line. It would be a violation of good taste to actually sing the texts with the music, yet there would be the same validity involved in printing the poetry on programs as in furnishing translations of texts in *Lieder* recitals. Actually, the composers expected their listeners to be familiar with these poems, for they were all quite celebrated in that era, and the motto was really meant only to refresh the memory. Under such terms, the duality of the esthetic experience was encompassed rather spontaneously. The compositions were meant to stand on their own merits and to be equally enjoyable with or without the poetry. This last point is an important one which is often lost sight of in discussions of literary-oriented music. The complete credo of the genre (and of program music in general) is to be found in "Berlioz and His 'Harold' Symphony," an essay written by Liszt as a defense of the Berlioz work.[3]

LISZT'S PIANO MUSIC WITH DESCRIPTIVE TITLES

Up to this point the discussion of Liszt's piano music has been concerned with *poetic* music. Before turning to a discussion of *descriptive* music, it must be pointed out that Liszt's *descriptive* works are seldom without some of the elements of the *poetic*, so that few of them are totally *descriptive* in nature. The *Études d'Exécution Transcendente* are an excellent example of varying degrees of program music. Of the complete set of twelve études, two have no titles at all, and are therefore assumed to be intended as abstract compositions in the étude tradition. Another is titled simply "Preludio" No. 1. Some, such as "Paysage" No. 3, are programmatic only in the most vaguely generalized terms; others are very descriptive, as "Feux Follets" and "Will-o'-the Wisps" (No. 5). "Mazeppa" depicts the daemonic ride and death song of Victor Hugo's hero, intensified by continually rising stages of rhythmic and technical agitation. In spite of the programmatic demands, its form is a theme and variations that has been worked out in an extremely logical and methodical fashion. The formal structuring serves to heighten the effect, a technical feat which illustrates one of the cardinal points of Liszt's credo—that program and abstract form can create an effective union and not just a distressing combination.[4] A more complex form is displayed in "*Wilde Jagd*" (No. 8), where three themes are combined to build to a pyrotechnical finale: the *Wilde Jagd* theme proper, a syncopated figure, the hunting horn theme, and the "enchanting song of the young witches," all of which are woven together as a fantastic night ride in the spirit of the *Walpurgis* episode in *Faust.*

Liszt has contributed some important works as a musical nature poet. This group of piano pieces includes "Album d'un Voyageur" which is divided into three volumes: (1) *Impressions et Poésies,* (2) *Fleurs mélodiques des Alpes,* and (3) *Paraphrases* (of Swiss melodies). The revised edition of these pieces became known as *Années de Pèlerinage.* As a musical painter of landscape pictures, Liszt has composed some of the greatest masterpieces in the genre: "Au lac de Wallenstadt," "Au bord d'une source," and "*Waldesrauschen.*" These are perennial favorites that have survived even the shift in modern taste toward abstraction.

LISZT'S PIANO TRANSCRIPTIONS

In the role of virtuoso Liszt realized a much more versatile range of operations than Paganini. As an educator, Liszt not only formed a subsidiary staff of piano teachers who then prepared students for inspirational private lessons with the master, but he also pioneered in the presentation of new works of other composers. Not content with featuring only new piano compositions, he also reached out into the new orchestral and operatic fields by making transcriptions. Just as Paganini had probed the technical and tonal possibilities of the violin, Liszt now set about an active exploration of the possibilities of the newly-improved pianoforte. For this purpose, and the sake of entertaining his audiences with familiar as well as new materials, he transcribed from every possible medium: songs, symphonies, organ works, operas, overtures, and popular tunes. These transcriptions range from potpourris, such as *Reminiscences de Puritani* (Bellini) to complete and faithfully rendered integral compositions, such as Berlioz's *Symphonie Fantastique.* Close examination of the potpourris reveals a remarkable degree of insight into basic thematic, dramatic, and key relationships, as in the famous *Reminiscence de Don Juan* (after Mozart). Such compositions anticipate, to an astounding degree, the forms of his later symphonic poems. Analyses of the strictly orchestral renderings—although written for the piano—reveal an admirable synthesis of orchestral colors and sonorities.

PIANISTIC EFFECTS IN LISZT'S ORCHESTRAL SCORES

By a curious process of reciprocal action Liszt transferred orchestral sonorities to the keyboard in his transcriptions, and when he began to compose orchestral works, transferred keyboard techniques into his scores. Precisely these pianistic transplants account for most of Liszt's many contributions to modern orchestral sound. Extended arpeggiated figurations for harp, as in *Les Préludes* (No. 97), are obvious, but their real significance lies in the extent of their use. More daring experimentation carried the arpeggio into string and woodwind parts, and in the following example from the *Faust Symphony* (No. 108), the arpeggiated parts even move in rhythms of two against three in a pianistic manner:

Example 1. Liszt, *Faust-Symphony,* Third Movement, Measure 506.

In *Faust,* the opening theme of the first movement has a pianistic cast in its use of augmented triads. Similarly, the viola accompaniment of the "Gretchen" theme in the slow movement of *Faust* has a singularly pianistic figuration. Reduction to oboe melody and viola accompaniment is strikingly similar to writing for the right and left hand of the piano.

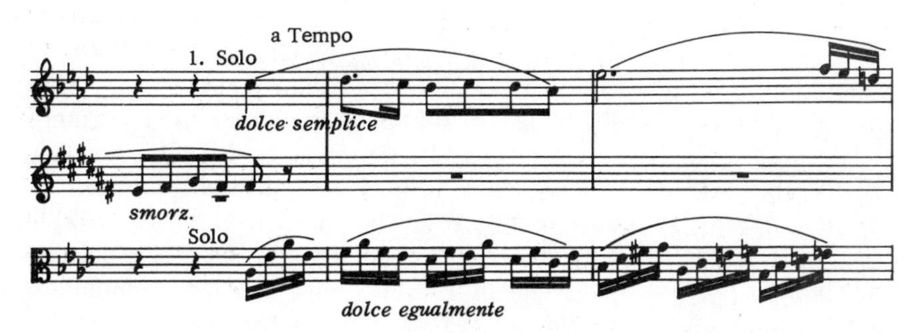

Example 2. Liszt, *Faust-Symphony,* Second Movement, Measures 15-17.

THE PIANO SONATA IN B MINOR

Liszt's great *Piano Sonata in B Minor, Raabe* No. 178, is a fusion of several musical elements into a structural whole of wonderful complexity. It is, first of all, such a successful fusion of the pianistic and orchestral sound that one ceases to think in terms of borrowed elements and accepts it as a sound complex on its own terms. Likewise, it is also a fusion of the sonata-allegro form with the form of the symphonic poem with which Liszt had been experimenting extensively. On the one hand, then, it is a further development of Beethoven's latest sonatas and an attempt to idealize the traditional form by breaking down the barriers of separate movements in order to form a self-generating whole. On the other hand, it is a development of the principle of *thematic transformation,* attempting a cyclic unity of thematic materials. The symphonic poem, as Liszt developed it, depended upon two forces for its unity; the poetic idea or story, and the use of germinal motives which the composer could manipulate, through successive stages of *thematic transformation,* in order to express his poetic idea or illustrate the story. Essentially the technique of *thematic transformation* provides an effective agent for progress from states of active and demonstrative tensions to states of lyrical and passive feeling; in this sense it is an ideal agent for creating subtle gradients of tension. In the *B Minor Sonata,* Liszt has eliminated the explicit statement of a program, story, or poetic idea, yet when confronted by its highly dramatic juxtapositions of materials, one is left with the uneasy feeling that something is missing. Of course, nothing is missing except an accustomed association of the "Liszt sound" with programmatic content. This association builds on some very famous precedents in the *Quasi una Fantasia* Sonatas, Op. 27, Nos. 1 and 2 of Beethoven, and the *Wanderer Fantasy* of Schubert, but surpasses them in the demonstration of versatility with germinal themes.

LISZT'S SYMPHONIC POEMS

Liszt's thirteen symphonic poems represent an extremely broad range of topical interests. Five were inspired by poems (Nos. 1, 2, 3, 6, and 12), and one by a play in blank verse (No. 10). Two were inspired by paintings (Nos. 11 and 13), and two were intended as overtures to plays (Nos. 2 and 10). In total, they point up the important cultural influences of his life; those emanating from French sources are numbers 1, 3, 4, 6, and 8; those emanating from the Weimar court circle are numbers 2, 5, 7, 10, and 12; and those stemming from his native country are numbers 9 and 11. It should be noted that another very significant influence in his life, the church, is not represented at all.

These thirteen symphonic poems vary greatly in degrees of programmatic narrative content. Some are based upon extremely general poetic ideas, others upon rather complete narrative stories, and still others upon simple pictorial content. All, however, have poetic content of some kind, although this may have been less germane to Liszt's musical thinking than it appears to us to be. Other musical concepts appear with much more uniform regularity. All, for instance, fuse the basic ideas of form in symphony, overture, and fantasy. Likewise, all are conceived as works in a single movement, subdivided into sections that are connected without pauses. Most important, all exhibit the principle of *thematic transformation,* some in a highly economical manner and the others in varying degrees of consistency. This latter quality appears to be largely influenced by the number of basic themes chosen for development. In *Les Préludes,* one germinal theme suffices, and from it all materials are derived by alteration of time, tempo, or contour. In fact, this is the almost too perfect example of *thematic transformation,* except that the monothematic plan is most appropriate to the poetic thought. Lamartine's poem expresses the thought that life is but a series of "Preludes" to death: the germinal theme observes the poem's singleness of vision.

Suggested Listening Assignments

1. Liszt, Franz: *Faust Symphony.* In what ways does the composer link the three movements together? How is musical form treated in the various movements?

2. LISZT, FRANZ: *Piano Sonata in B Minor.* Listen to the theme of the slow introduction, the "fertilizing germ" for the four principal themes of the sonata to come. Can you hear this relationship? Is this work rather free and rhapsodic or closely unified?

SUGGESTED ADDITIONAL LISTENING ASSIGNMENTS

1. LISZT, FRANZ: *The Preludes.* In what ways is this a perfect example of thematic transformation? Can you make out the various sections of a possible sonata allegro form?
2. LISZT, FRANZ: *Mazeppa.* Read a translation of Hugo's poem of the same name. Can you relate the contents of the poem to this music? Is the relationship literal, or only a general impression of the poem?

SUGGESTED READING ASSIGNMENTS

CbT pp. 372-375
EaM pp. 140-149
FdA pp. 434-440
GdA pp. 519-521; 538-539
HaM pp. 835-850
LpM pp. 864-873
ScO pp. 297-299
UhA pp. 494-499

SUGGESTED WRITTEN ASSIGNMENTS

1. Discuss the relationship existing between poetry and music which is present in one or several of Liszt's symphonic poems.
2. Discuss the element of *expansion* in nineteenth-century culture with respect to (a) music in its own right; (b) music in connection with poetry; (c) music outside the rules of the school (or tradition); (d) music in relation to the music of future generations.
3. Some would like to see in Liszt the Romanticist *par excellence.* Do you agree? Consider his life with respect to (a) political movements; (b) theories of social reform; (c) freedom of movement and travel; (d) relationship to employers; (e) feeling of brotherhood to man; (f) importance of love and friendship.

FOOTNOTES

[1]ShS, p. 80
[2]ShS, p. 84
[3]SwS, p. 847
[4]SwS, p. 852

chapter 10

the music drama: wagner

WAGNER'S LITERARY WRITINGS

Romantic fusion of literature and music reaches its climax in Richard Wagner. His many very brilliant talents qualified him extremely well to meet the challenges posed by the earlier Romantic composers, particularly Liszt and Berlioz, and to strike out toward new concepts. He distinguished himself as one of the greatest letter writers among musicians, both as to quality and quantity, and he was also an important essayist on philosophy, politics, and music. To these strengths he added his enormous creativity in music; indeed, he can be credited with the formulation of the modern music drama and its concepts of *leitmotive,* continuous melody, and musical and dramatic homogeneity.

OPERA AND DRAMA (1851)

Traditional opera has often been called a "fool's paradise for all the absurdities in the world." This is because opera has allowed music to become an end in itself and has used drama only as a means to that end. In the future this situation must be changed, and the drama must be brought into congruence with the music. In the selection of themes, myths will serve as an important vehicle, because they can be used as a means of poetic simplification or condensation which allows the poet to make one person on the stage represent a composite of innumerable individuals. Taken in this sense, the myth becomes a representation of the most ultimate reality because it presents the best possible abstraction of existing psychological conditions. The abstractions themselves can be represented by musical motives, to be known later as *leitmotives,* symbolically representing the unutterable inward thoughts of the characters on stage, and thus indicating the subconscious origin of various actions otherwise inexpressed through the spoken word (or speech-tone).

THE LEITMOTIVE

Leitmotives, literally leading themes, were used by Wagner to symbolize characters, objects, and ideas. They appear in vocal and orchestral parts, but primarily in the orchestra, where they give added meaning to the action on the stage. Wagner's use of the *leitmotive* developed slowly. In the early operas the motives have more of a musical purpose, while in the *Ring* their use is primarily psychological and dramatic. In fact, they have the same external and internal mobility and drive as dramatic motives. They cause action as well as represent it. In this way they are very different from other motives.

The *Leitmotive* is related to the idée fixe of Berlioz and the French *reminiscence motive.* All of these devices derive from Baroque recitative accompaniments in which little motives interrupt the recitative. These motives portray the gesture of the actor on the stage, but they are not musically related to the vocal part and they are not repeated. In Wagner's music dramas these expressive motives are no longer mere interjections interrupting the flow of dramatic action. Instead, by much repetition, and by greatly expanded sequences based upon the motives, large forms and psychological structures are created.

He does not use the development principle of the symphonists. A *leitmotive* is never as clearly and precisely defined as a symphonic theme. It is much more like a nucleus which is in motion. The *leitmotive* technique is of much greater simplicity. Its value lies in this simplicity and in the great variability of statement of the motif. The Ring motive, for example, is an energetic moving center, about which co-motives constantly revolve.

Example 1. Wagner, *Das Rheingold,* First Scene, Ring-motive.

Example 2. Wagner, *Das Rheingold,* Second Scene, Valhalla-motive.

Example 3. Wagner, *Das Rheingold,* First Scene, Nature-motive.

Actually there are not single motives, but many statements of a motivic germ. Everything is based upon interchange and variability.

WAGNER AND THE LIBRETTO

Wagner's libretti, all of which came from his own pen, display a remarkable skill in the handling of dramatic situations. They contain an endless variety of patterns of meter, rhyme, and versification, sensitively chosen to contribute to character differentiation and dramatic fidelity. In *Tannhäuser,* for example, the *Sirens* in Act I, Scene 2, are given a meter based upon five syllables to the line. Tannhäuser's lines, however, alternate between eleven and twelve syllables to the line.

By contrast, the famous *Rome Narration* in Scene 3 of the same Act is written in prose instead of in poetic meter. The complete "narration" is separated into nine different sections. While the first section can be easily identified, the later sections follow each other in almost uninterrupted fashion, making them less easily differentiable as the dramatic tension builds toward its climactic point.

WAGNER AS INNOVATOR IN SYMPHONY INSTRUMENTS

Wagner figured in the development of several lower range brass instruments: the trombone, the contra-bass trombone, the bass tuba, and the "Wagner" tuba. The trombone had been in use for a long time before Wagner, particularly in the opera orchestra, but it was seldom given anything to accord it real prominence in its own right, as in the *Ride of Valkyries* in the *Ring.* The contra-bass trombone was also in use before Wagner took an interest in it. It was a two-slide instrument with one slide doubled back parallel to the other. It made available certain low tones previously impossible on the tenor and bass trombones. Although Wagner used it in several of his works, it was most notably utilized to its full capacity in the *Ring*. The bass tuba was developed as a replacement for the bass trombone. Wagner used it principally in his early works, such as *Faust* and the *Flying Dutchman*. The "Wagner" tubas were invented by the composer especially for use in the *Ring* to fill the gap between the French horns and trombones. Used in sets of four, they were similar to the modern euphonium, but a little larger, and there was less forward tilt to the bell.

WAGNER AND COLORISTIC ORCHESTRATION

Wagner's powers of instrumental stylization were so great that even the individual operas of the *Ring* have their own particular sound. Strauss voiced this reaction by saying that every Wagnerian work had its own unique orchestra.[2]

The Wagnerian orchestral art does not consist merely of volume added upon volume, in fact, it frequently achieves a quality of the closest kind of intimacy. This may be seen in *Lohengrin*.[3]

The unique role of the woodwinds in *Lohengrin* is the result of a dominating *poetic idea* which prescribes the instrumental style of the entire opera. Strauss refers specifically to the imitative sound of the organ and its effect upon the poetic atmosphere. The organ quality is obtained by mixing combinations of woodwinds in a manner somewhat analogous to organ mixture stops, and the resulting sound is considerably more flexible than the straight organ sound would be. An excellent example of this is afforded by the woodwind treatment immediately following the male chorus, "Behold, she comes, the maid suspected," in Act I, Scene 2. This portion consists of an eight-measure musical period with two four-measure phrases. Even though the first phrase is marked *piano* and *sehr zart* (*dolcissimo*), the woodwinds are doubled, the three flute parts by two B-flat clarinets and first bassoon. Obviously, the doubling is not done in order to reinforce the volume of sound, but rather to change its color, slightly displacing the flute-clarinet sound by one which suggests the organ sonority. It should be noted that the oboe is not used in combination, for its tone would not too easily penetrate as straight oboe sound, too individual for the combination. In a process such as this, part of the individuality of an instrument is lost through doubling, but there has been a distinct gain in total orchestral sound. In Wagner's hands, these techniques make the orchestra into a more expressive and adaptive tool.

WAGNER'S ORCHESTRATION AS A PART OF HIS COMPOSITIONAL TECHNIQUE

Wagner's manipulation of instrumental coloration coincides with his attempt to achieve an uninterrupted, continuous stream of music whose motives, phrases, and periods are all fused into one integrated whole. The most familiar work in which this technique is used throughout is *Tristan,* but our example from *Lohengrin* (above) provides just as classic an example of this structural and instrumental *Verschmelzungstechnik* (technique of melting-together). Here, the end of the first four-bar phase coincides wtih the beginning of the second phrase. The overlapping is done in such a way that only a part of the instrumentation of the first phrase will sound against the beginning of the second phrase. In our example only the flutes, *pianissimo,* remain to sound against the oboes, English horn, and bassoons, *piano,* at the beginning of the second phrase. At the moment of the instrumental transfer (Umschlag), the sound of the flutes melts into the other instruments in such a subtle fashion that no break is experienced, and all that can be distinguished is a new inflection of the sound in the musical continuity. The melodic structure is likewise executed in an analogous technique. Phrase one is a variation of phrase two (actually the B section of an AABA formation) a half-step higher, the two being joined by a dominant seventh chord. Thus, orchestration, harmony, and melody all assist in forming the chain of structural integration.

Suggested Listening Assignments

1. Wagner, Richard: *Das Rheingold.* Listen to the three leitmotives given in the text. Try to hear them in the texture of the music of *Das Rheingold.* Try to make out as many restatements of these motives as possible. Is the reappearance of the motives in agreement with the dramatic action? In what ways?
2. Wagner, Richard: *Tannhäuser, Act III, Scene 3.* Listen to the nine sections of the Rome narration as described in the text. How does the orchestra contribute to dramatic intensification? Are we already in the presence of a concept of a "symphony with accompanying vocal parts" rather than an operatic vocal section with accompanying instrumental parts? Are there any motives which play a major role?
3. Wagner, Richard: *Lohengrin, Act I, Scene 2.* Listen to this music, following the description in the text.

Suggested Reading Assignments

CbT pp. 376-393
EaM pp. 226-255
FdA pp. 477-498
GdA pp. 561-567
HaM pp. 743-758
LpM pp. 873-894
ScO pp. 288-293
UhA pp. 531-540

Suggested Written Assignments

1. Discuss the Germanic quality in Wagner's works with respect to (a) topics of operas; (b) relationship to employers; (c) Wagner and Beethoven.
2. Discuss Wagner's influence on other composers with respect to (a) melodic treatment; (b) harmonic language; (c) orchestral technique; (d) length of musical compositions; (e) expressive quality.
3. How does the "erotic" quality in the prelude to *Tristan and Isolde* come through musically? Do the harmonic progressions help to create this effect? Is the orchestration a decisive factor?
4. What "Romantic" traits, as discussed in preceding chapters, can be found in Wagner's works?
5. Discuss the literary sources of the *Ring*.

Footnotes

[1]EuF, p. 79
[2]SrH, p. III
[3]SrH, p. II

part IV

MUSIC OF VARIOUS NATIONS

chapter 11

italy

NINETEENTH-CENTURY ITALIAN OPERA

During many centuries Italian music maintained in every form the genuine expression of a national art. Through the opera, Italian musicians colonized most of Europe during the seventeenth and eighteenth centuries, and they retained a position of leadership in this field throughout the nineteenth century. None of the Italian musicians of the Baroque era brought home the mark of a foreign, i.e., of a German, a French, or a Russian style, and it was characteristic that Giuseppe Verdi (1813-1901), a Romantic era composer, wrote his opera *Aïda* for the opening of an *Italian* opera theater in Cairo (1871). This same Verdi, however, effected successfully in his time the merger of various national styles—French with Italian in the opera *Don Carlos* and German with Italian in the late Shakespeare-Boito operas *Othello* and *Falstaff*.

During the seventeenth and eighteenth centuries Italian composers had helped to develop such important forms as the concerto grosso, the sonata, and the symphony, but in the nineteenth century the preeminence of instrumental music in Italy declined. (As late as 1876 the only copy of Beethoven's symphonies that could be found was at the library of the Conservatory in Milan, and it was so full of mistakes as to be in some parts unintelligible.) In its stead, opera completely dominated the local musical scene, becoming the best propagandist of the general temper of the Italian *Risorgimiento* (1818-1848). During this time, opera was mainly appreciated not in its own right, but rather for the sake of expressing the passions aroused by the tumultuous, picturesque, and Romantic adventure of Italian unification. While the eighteenth-century opera-goer admired primarily the technical abilities of the singers, nineteenth-century Italian audiences wanted to identify themselves with the characters on the stage, to become personally involved in heroic sacrifice, candid devotion, and outrageous violence committed in the name of patriotism and nationalism.

VARIOUS INFLUENCES ON OPERA WRITING

Audience-involved opera did not, however, originate in Italy, but appeared first in those countries where a great dramatic tradition already existed. There was little of such a tradition in eighteenth-century Italy, but a very strong one in eighteenth-century France in the works of Corneille, Racine, Molière, and Voltaire; so it was that this type of opera came to Italy via France. Furthermore, the reform movement of Gluck, never entirely forgotten in France, was still strong enough to influence nineteenth-century operas. Thus, the Italians Cherubini and Spontini had to compete with French national composers and to adjust to French needs and tastes. The Gluck reforms can also be traced in other Italians such as Antonio Sacchini (1730-1786) and Antonio Salieri (1750-1825).

Gluck's influence was brought to Italy by an Italianized Bavarian, Simon Mayr (1763-1845), one of the last distinguished opera composers before Rossini's rise to fame in 1813. Mayr introduced a type of choral opera which had its roots in Gluck's work, and adjusted German instrumental innovations to the Italian taste, surprising his listeners with many modern effects. His musical influence, extended by his famous pupil, Donizetti, was as powerful as that of Rossini.

ROSSINI

Along with its essential reaction to *bourgeois* Romanticism, Rossini's art embodied, in the midst of renewed political agitations, the ideal of the Restoration and a nostalgia for the *belle époque.* In accordance with the need for relaxation and repose that was felt all over Europe after the Napoleonic wars, he endeavored to restore the tradition of Italian opera, and his music fascinated people with its rhythmic energy, its robust instrumental sound, and its superb melodic quality. The youthful *Cyrus in Babylon* (1812) represents his adaptation of Mayr's choral opera style; he continued along these lines in *Moses* (1818) and *Semiramide* (1823). In contrast to eighteenth-century practice, Rossini wrote out all vocal embellishments.

Like Napoleon, Rossini was a conqueror. His first conquest was Italy, which at that time was divided into two musico-geographic areas, the famous Neapolitan school in the south, and the opera schools of the north in Milan, Venice, and Bologna. These latter cities were won with *Tancredi* and *An Italian in Algiers*. The *Gazette* and *Othello* were signals of his victory in Naples. Rossini's operas thus helped to unify the two sectors of Italian musical life and at the same time reestablished the predominance of Italian opera.

Three types of *opera buffa* were cultivated around the turn of the nineteenth century: (1) the entirely comic *opera buffa*, or *opera farsa*; (2) the *dramma giocoso*, in which serious parts were added to the comic opera; and (3) the *opera semiseria*, or sentimental opera (*comédie larmoyante*). Rossini excelled in all three types. *An Italian in Algiers* is an *opera farsa; The Barber of Seville, The Happy Deception*, and *Cinderella* are examples of *dramma giocoso*; *The Thieving Magpie* is an *opera semiseria*. With these works, Rossini brought the long-standing Italian *opera buffa* tradition to a triumphant finale.

In the realm of *opera seria*, however, Rossini not only renewed eighteenth-century style but went beyond it. This was accomplished in *The Siege of Corinth* (a revision of *Mahomet II*, Naples, 1820), *Moses in Egypt* (a revision of *Moses in Egypt*, Naples, 1818), and *William Tell*. These revised operas along with *William Tell* were first produced in Paris, 1827-1829. Rossini had reformed the genre by (1) constructing numbers more broadly, using extended and audacious harmonic schemes; (2) by making the role of the orchestra larger and more symphonic; (3) by giving more importance to the chorus; (4) by making accompaniments more vigorous and vivid, and (5) by using reminiscence motives extensively, anticipating the Wagnerian *leitmotive* technique. (This last device, especially prominent in *William Tell*, was foreshadowed in *Semiramide*.) All of these reforms had considerable influence on the development of French grand opera, as exemplified particularly by Meyerbeer's *Robert the Devil*.

The second *Moses* (Paris, 1827) is more than a translation and adaptation of the first. In the Paris version, Rossini omitted three regular arias, two conventional and concerted *stretta*, and a short chorus. He added an overture, three extended ensemble scenes, and one dramatic, unconventional aria. The revision thus contains only two arias, one for each of the sopranos, and both are actively interrupted and enriched by appeals and interjections from other characters and from the chorus. We see, then, in these works an unexpected feeling for the music drama of the kind praised in Gluck and in the mature Verdi.

The curious result was that Rossini, regarded as an innovator in Italy, was considered a conservative in France.

BELLINI AND DONIZETTI

Between Rossini and Verdi there was an interregnum, largely presided over by Bellini and Donizetti, two highly Romantic composers whose ultimate musical goal was a *cantabile* quality. They translated emotions into song, as it were. Their Italian brand of Romanticism was dedicated neither to nature nor to some form of transcendentalism, but found its expression in love-usually unhappy, consuming and sometimes consumptive—love very different from that portrayed in *Faust,* for example, or *Tristan.* Exploiting this Romantic attitude, the operas of Bellini and Donizetti portray individuals devoured by this consuming passion. In Donizetti's operas, to illustrate, we find such characters as Anne Boleyn, Torquato Tasso, Lucrezia Borgia, Marie Stuart, and Lucia de Lammermoor, persons with whose destinies Italian middle-class audiences were much more able to identify, rather than with, for example, those of the Semiramides of eighteenth-century plots.

The careers of Bellini and Donizetti confirmed the decline of the Neapolitan school of opera and of "Rossini-ism," and helped to create a unification of national taste under pressures brought to bear by the schools of northern Italy, which were more cosmopolitan and therefore more receptive to French and German influences.

VERDI

Around 1830-1840 Italy's political awakening to the ideals of national liberation changed the goals of operatic writing. The love operas of Bellini and Donizetti no longer sufficed. Something new was demanded, something virile and heroic, something which could reflect the political enthusiasms of Italian youth. Giuseppe Mazzini, founder of a political association called "Young Italy" (1831), in his *Filosofia della Musica* (1836), asked for musical drama, ennoblement of the recitative, development of choral parts, and more intensive study of instrumentation. Furthermore, he wanted music to go beyond individualism to discover "God and the People."

The operas of Verdi became the "Voice of the People," and in creating this Voice, Verdi proceeded along four broad paths.

1. He continued the choral opera tradition of Mayr. He was attracted to this type, but faced difficulties of a practical nature in that few opera houses of that time were able to afford the kind of expensive

staging and production required by these operas. Having had to deal with provincial houses during his youth, Verdi could not afford to continue writing choral operas after his initial successes with *Nabucco* (1842) and *The Lombards* (1843).

2. He turned to libretti which clearly reflected the concepts of personal and national liberty, strong and idealistic humanitarianism, and detestation for royal and aristocratic privilege. Verdi realized these ideals operatically in four works (*Joan of Arc,* 1845; *The Robbers,* 1847; *Louisa Miller,* 1849; *Don Carlos,* 1865-67), based on texts by Schiller, whose own abhorrence of tyranny is plainly seen in his dramatic poem, *William Tell.* It is significant that the first three are grouped around 1848, the period during which the European governments set up by Metternich at the Congress of Vienna fought their last battles against democratic movements. The last of Verdi's Schiller operas, *Don Carlos,* was written much later and is probably the most rewarding of all the works written in the style of French grand opera. Here are found the big choruses, spectacular scenes, fanfare motives, triplets, and pompous dotted notes characteristic of the style that Meyerbeer had introduced thirty years earlier in his Parisian operas.

3. After political disappointments, Verdi turned to psychological themes. *Rigoletto* (1851), *The Trovatore,* and *La Traviata* (both 1853), completed an operatic type which he had begun with *Ernani* (1844). In the period extending from *The Italian Vespers* (1855) to *Aïda* (1871), Verdi's musical dramatism became richer and more mature. He approached the dramatic ideals that he had always envisioned and which were finally attained in his last works, the two Shakespeare operas.

4. *Othello* (1887) and *Falstaff* (1892-93) are considered by many to show a proximity to the style of Wagnerian music drama. In *Othello,* Wagner's influence can be seen in (1) the closeness with which the music follows the word; (2) the relaxation of form and departure from traditional Italian melody; and (3) the orchestral effects from strings and woodwinds (also seen in earlier works, e.g., the prelude to *Traviata*). The introductory tempest chorus of *Othello,* known as the greatest musical description of nature ever written by Verdi, is a passage of outstanding beauty. Tone painting effects are also very apparent in the subsequent bonfire chorus. In *Othello,* then, Verdi created a *scenic drama for music* which is continuous and flowing, with neither pauses for recitativi nor cadences for applause (unusual omittances for Italian opera), a drama whose incidents are blended together just as is Shakespeare's uninterrupted verse. It is not so much Wagner's, but rather Mendelssohn's influence that can be detected in the orchestral techniques and in the motives of the "Elf's Scene" (Act III, Scene 2) of

Falstaff. Polyphonic writing of the highest order is, however, the outstanding musical element of this opera, and the final *buffa* fugue, "Tutto nel mondo e burla" (Everything in the world is a joke), is a masterpiece.

Example 1. Verdi, *Falstaff,* Excerpt from the final fugue.

Suggested Listening Assignments

1. Rossini, Gioacchino: *The Barber of Seville.* What is the *buffa* element in the instrumental and vocal sections of this *dramma giocoso?* What is the Italian quality of this work? (Listen to melody, rhythm, harmony, orchestration.)
2. Verdi, Giuseppe: *Don Carlos.* Listen for the qualities of the French grand opera as described in the text.
3. Verdi, Giuseppe: *La Traviata.* Listen for the arias and ensembles.

Suggested Additional Listening Assignments

1. Bellini, Vincenzo: *Norma.* Listen for the "simplicity and naturalness" which are characteristics of the arias. Do the arias communicate with you? Are they obsolete?
2. Rossini, Gioacchino: *William Tell.* What is the outstanding quality of this opera? Listen for the handling of choral parts.
3. Verdi, Giuseppe: *Falstaff.* How does Verdi's melodic gift come to the foreground? Describe his orchestration. How does he achieve continuity?

Suggested Reading Assignments

EaM pp. 262-286
FdA pp. 470-473; 513-517
GdA pp. 550-557
HaM pp. 782-802
LpM pp. 834-839; 909-915
ScO pp. 294-296
UhA pp. 455-458; 524-530

Suggested Written Assignments

1. Compare Rossini's overture to *William Tell* with the equally famous two preludes (Act I and Act III) from Verdi's *La Traviata.*
2. List the literary sources of all Verdi operas mentioned in this chapter. Draw whatever conclusions you can and compare with other nineteenth-century opera composers such as Weber, Wagner, etc.
3. Describe a musical pilgrimage to Milan where most of Verdi's operas still obtain their most brilliant interpretations.

chapter 12

france

FOREIGN INFLUENCES

The French *salon* of the eighteenth century was revived after 1815 by the restored nobility, and it was in these gatherings of aristocracy and intelligentsia that two great foreign musicians, Franz Liszt (1811-1886) and Frédéric Chopin (1810-1849), made their Paris debuts in 1824 and 1832, respectively. The success of two piano virtuosi thus made the French receptive to the music of other foreigners, the most important of whom were Weber, Beethoven, Rossini, Meyerbeer, Wagner, and Jacques Offenbach (1819-1880).

Weber and Beethoven

Weber's *Der Freischütz* (1821), with the popular cast of its choruses and dances and by the originality of its orchestration, made a particularly strong impression on Berlioz, so much that sections of his own *Damnation of Faust* (1846) are fashioned after Weber's famous "Wolf Glen" scene. Beethoven's influence was transmitted through the Parisian conductor, François Antoine Habeneck (1781-1849), an outstanding leader who, beginning in 1828, performed in succession the nine symphonies of the German master. By 1830 Habeneck had reached the *Pastorale,* and it was here that Berlioz first became acquainted with this work, distinct echoes of which were later to appear in his *Symphonie Fantastique* (1831).

Rossini and Meyerbeer

Rossini represents one source of Italian influence during this period. He had worked in Paris with the Italian Theater since 1817, then had obtained a position at the French court in 1824 and retained it up to the Revolt of 1830. Prominent literary figures such as Stendhal, Musset, and Balzac loved his music, but other French Romantics, namely Hugo, Lamartine, and the painter Delacroix, refused to join in the adulation. Berlioz, having apparently overlooked the pure Romantic nuances in the famous *William Tell,* also shared this critical attitude.

Scene from Auber's **"La Muette De Portici,"** 1828. (Important Grand Opera, together with Rossini's **"William Tell."**)

Meyerbeer, the last great opera composer who went to Italy to learn his craft before the tide changed and flowed toward Bayreuth, was destined to leave a lasting impression on French music. After early Italian successes, he went on to Paris and spent seven years preparing his first French triumph, *Robert the Devil* (1831), which was followed by the equally successful works *The Huguenots* (1836) and *The Prophet* (1849). Heine, Gautier, and others attacked Meyerbeer for his compromising attitude, for always seeking the *right milieu* or whatever was acceptable at the moment. In reality, this was not a negative but rather a positive attribute, for he wrote true *contemporary* music. His operas dealt with the problems of his time and he dramatized situations by painting their participants solely in black and white.

Wagner and Offenbach

Two other foreign composers, Wagner and Offenbach, had a remarkable influence on French music in the nineteenth century. The tale of Wagner's encounters with the Parisian public was far from a success story, for he experienced many rebuffs, and his music was only grudgingly introduced. Yet his operas, despite their piecemeal introduction (they were not produced in full until the eighties and nineties), had an enormous impact on musicians and other artists as well. The dissemination, for example, of Wagner's theories of art stimulated French painters to conceive painting as music in colors, and poets such as Mallarmé, Verlaine, and Baudelaire to think of poetry as music. Among the many French composers who made the pilgrimage to Bayreuth were Vincent d'Indy (1851-1931), Henri Duparc (1848-1933), Emmanuel Chabrier (1841-1894), and Debussy. Debussy wrote of *Parsifal* ". . . [it is] one of the most beautiful monuments of music which have been raised to the imperturbable glory of music." Having then some idea of the extent of Wagner's influence on French art, and thus by definition on French life, it is indeed more understandable how a nation that had just experienced the bitter Franco-Prussian War of 1870-71 could, in 1885, give birth in Paris to the *Wagnerian Review.*

Offenbach's operettas, numbering more than one hundred, are especially interesting in that they were written for specific theaters where he was musical director—theaters which were in many ways related to the burlesque. These are all works of *double entendre,* full of criticism of the society for which he wrote. Those who, in all good faith, take the *Tales of Hoffman* as only Hoffman's tales miss the point completely. In his ability to criticize and entertain at the same time, Offenbach foreshadows Kurt Weill (1900-1950), of *Threepenny Opera* fame.

During the Restoration and Post-Restoration Eras, then, music in France eventually became an art which sought to please everybody. The expression of national, political, and social aspirations through music was felt to be of little importance, and mere entertainment seemed its principal goal. These years of superficiality saw, however, the founding of the *Conservatory of Music* and the *Société des Concerts,* and other signs of a Renaissance, and a return to sensitivity appeared.

AFTER 1870: THE FRENCH RENAISSANCE

There were several reasons for this Renaissance of French music during the last quarter of the century. Chief among them may be cited: (1) the military defeat of 1871, and the consequent reawakening of national conscience; (2) the growing antagonism to the materialism of grand opera; and (3) the concern felt for French composers and performers.

National Influences: Neoclassicism

The strongest nationalistic influence on the "Rebirth" came from remembering the French musical classicism of the preceding century, and French composers now revived the ideals of Couperin and Rameau, concentrating on structural balance, moderation, and clarity. Emphasis on classic concepts led directly to the very French music of Debussy's last sonatas, which, notwithstanding the presence of impressionistic techniques, represent Neoclassicism *par excellence.*

National Influences: Use of Folklorical Materials

A second national factor was the folk-song revival in France, which paralleled similar movements in other countries. Scholarly studies and collections had considerable influence on d'Indy's *Symphonie Cévenole* (1886), and extended even to some of Debussy's piano works—*Gardens in the Rain,* for example, uses a folk song as its basic melodic material. French composers turned also to the folk music of other countries, as is evidenced by the titles of such works as *Algerian Suite* (Saint-Saens), *Hungarian Scenes* (Massenet), and *Norwegian Rhapsody* (Lalo).

National Influences: The Poètes Parnassiens and Other Artists

During this period, the *Poètes Parnassiens,* the Symbolists, and the Impressionistic painters had great influence on music in France. The close relationship between poetry and painting helped to change the forms and the aesthetic goals of music. A case in point, Debussy related to the Pointillist painters in his adaptation of their techniques for his orchestrations, and to the Symbolist writers in his use of their texts for his songs. Indeed, his transcendence of all art forms could be considered a national trait.

The Materialism of Grand Opera

Although the grand operas of Meyerbeer were only a small part of the output of a flourishing lyric theater, they were nevertheless the expression of a materialistic way of thinking, and one commentator, Victor de Laprade, even called the *Opéra* a "cathedral of materialism." Charles Gounod (1818-1893) continued the grand style, but discarded some of its bombastic and monumental elements. His *Faust* (1859) represented a praiseworthy attempt to free French opera from the Meyerbeer-Rossini tradition. In the operas of Georges Bizet (1838-1875), simple and folklike qualities, coupled with refreshing emphasis on rhythmic vitality, are stressed. Toward the end of the century, two variations on the traditional opera appeared. One is represented by the works of Gustave Charpentier (1860-1956), who set librettos by Zola to produce what might be called "naturalistic" operas. The other, based on the writings of the Symbolists, is best seen in Debussy's *Pelléas and Mélisande.* This unique opera has no big choruses, no duets or ensembles of any kind, nor even any climactic arias. The singing is primarily *recitativo* monologue or dialogue, and is accompanied by an orchestra that is not symphonic but chamber-like in scoring.

Concern for French Composers and Performers

Linked to and growing from the reawakening of national conscience mentioned previously, this movement to "do something" for the French musician was championed by the composer Camille Saint-Saëns (1835-1921). In order to assure the performance of contemporary French instrumental works, he founded, under the motto *Ars Gallica,* the *Société Nationale de Musique.*

IN SUMMARY: TWO ATTITUDES TOWARD MUSIC

So it was that there were two opposing attitudes toward music in late nineteenth-century France. The Romantics were set in opposition to the Neoclassicists, and the creators of art music were contrasted with those who wrote music destined only for entertainment. The most extreme representatives of the Romantic movement were Berlioz at the beginning of the period and César Franck (1822-1890) at the end. Among the Neoclassicists, likely choices would be Gounod and Saint-Saëns. Between these poles many composers—Édouard Lalo (1823-1892), Chabrier, Duparc, Ernest Chausson (1855-1899), d'Indy, and others—struck varying degrees of compromise.

Within the French Romantic movement, Berlioz and Franck form the most interesting contrast. In Berlioz there was the grandiose, the theatrical, the programmatic, but little of the abstract. Franck, by comparison, with his highly personal idiom in symphonic and chamber compositions, reestablished abstract Romantic music in France. Berlioz's mastery of portraying the diabolical was countered by an equally seraphic quality in the music of Franck. Finally, Berlioz founded no distinct school of composers, but Franck had many disciples who reflected his interest in counterpoint, fugue, cyclic forms, and variation techniques.

Suggested Listening Assignments

1. Meyerbeer, Giacomo: *The Huguenots.* Can you detect the composer's sense for the grandiose? Listen to the shape of the melodies, the nature of the chorus parts, their frequency, and the orchestration.
2. Offenbach, Jacques: *Tales of Hoffman.* Compare this with a Gilbert and Sullivan operetta; a Johann Strauss operetta. In what ways does it differ? In what ways is it similar?
3. Gounod, Charles: *Faust.* Listen to sections of this opera and compare the music with portions of Berlioz's *Damnation of Faust.*

Suggested Additional Listening Assignments

1. Franck, César: *Symphony in D Minor.* What are Franck's harmonic progressions like? Does he use chromaticism? Which movement is a showcase example of the cyclic form?
2. Bizet, Georges: *Carmen.* How does the sound of this opera differ from the sound of Meyerbeer's *The Huguenots*? How does the Spanish element appear in this opera?

Suggested Reading Assignments

EaM pp. 257-261; 286-292
FdA pp. 543-550
GdA pp. 546-550; 597-607
HaM pp. 913-922
LpM pp. 826-834; 923-929
UhA pp. 458-464; 500-505; 541-564; 578-582

Suggested Written Assignments

1. Write a little survey on the significance of César Franck's works.
2. Compare Bizet's *Carmen* with some of his other works.
3. Make a list of symphonies composed by nineteenth-century French composers.

chapter 13

russia

HISTORICAL PERIODS IN RUSSIAN MUSIC

Russia's Musical Self-Containment (-1600)

Russian music can be divided into five historical periods. The first, up to the end of the sixteenth century, resulted from the fact that Russia was culturally and politically isolated from western Europe and that it cultivated the tradition of eastern European art and music. During the time in which the art music of Gothic, Renaissance, and early Baroque style developed in western Europe, Russia's music consisted primarily of two traditions: church music and folk music. Although the folk music sometimes contained some crude polyphony, all of the sacred music was monophonic. Russian church music grew out of the Byzantine chant. Up to the thirteenth century it was sung in Greek and Slavic. Later, Slavic was the only language used. The long, undisturbed reign of church and folk music had its effect upon the sounds of later Russian art music, upon the vitality of the nationalistic movement in music in nineteenth-century Russia, and even upon the conservative attitude of twentieth-century Russian composers toward contemporary western techniques in music.

Contact with Western Music as Imposed by the Tsars (1600-1750)

The second period is characterized by Russia's gradual abandonment of her state of isolation. The approach to western materials can be seen in the imitation of western European three to four part faux-bourdon music, a compositional practice which was used by Russian folk singers before that time. The influence of Polish art music was also felt after 1650 in choral pieces built around a *cantus firmus.* The musical innovations under the tsar, Peter the Great (1682-1725), included the introduction of Baroque devices and choral hymns which were performed praising the institutions of the tsaristic empire. These were also combined with brass and performed in the theaters. We can still hear traces of their fanfarelike intradas and themes in Tchaikovsky's 1812 overture.

Impact of Western Music on Russian Music as a Whole (1750-1800)

The third period must be understood in the context of Russia's vast territorial expansion and her emergence as a great European power. This period is marked by the influence of western music upon all musical areas: upon opera, instrumental music, keyboard music, and the art song. Within a few years, under the influence of the enlightened Catherine II (1762-1796), some world famous Italian composers had taken up residence in Russia, such as Baldassare Galuppi (1706-1785) from 1763, Giovanni Paisiello (1740-1816) from 1776, and Domenico Cimarosa (1749-1801) from 1787. Italianate elements and national flavor, particularly in the choral writing, emerged in the comic Russian operas of Wassili Alexjewich Pashkevich (c. 1742-1800) ca. 1756 in his *Fedul and his Children* and in the operas of Ewestignej Ipatowich Fomin (1761-1800) in his *Miller, Sorcerer, Swindler* and *Matchmaker.*[2] The influence of western music was not confined to Italian music, however; a strong German and French influence was also noticeable.

Many operas describing the life of the Russian peasant and "petit bourgeois" were written during the latter half of the eighteenth century. The most important predecessor of the nationalistic composers of the nineteenth century was Dimitri Stepanovich Bortniansky (1751-1825). His music shows a remarkable synthesis of Italian and Russian elements. He wrote operas, sonatas, art songs, and a great quantity of church music. His "*Cherubic Hymn*" was the first sacred composition that could be purchased in a Russian music store (1782). The hymn is still sung throughout the world today.

Russia's Own Ballet and Art Song (1800-1850)

In the fourth period Russia caught up with the rest of Europe and crystalized her own musical idiom. Opera composers, many of whom belonged to literary societies, turned to such Russian figures as Pushkin, Gogol and Chekhov for libretti. The fight against Napoleon strengthened the interest in national folk tales and epics. The development of a classical national ballet in connection with the opera was begun by Charles Didelot in 1801. Ballerinas continued the soloistic performance tradition of the eighteenth-century singer. The ballet established a synthesis of national feeling, noticeable even in the works of Stravinsky, which makes Russian operas unthinkable without ballet.

The large repertoire of Russian art songs was established during that time. It developed from two contrasting traditions: the folk song, resulting in the anti-Romantic art songs of Modeste Petrovitch Mussorgsky (1839-1881), and the music of the "French" salons of Russia, resulting in the Romantic art songs of Tchaikovsky. The long Russian winters were a factor in the popularity of these middle-class salons, which fostered the development of literature and music. Alexander Ygorovitch Varlamoff (1801-1848) is the forerunner of the greater Russian art song composers. His romance, *The Red Sarafan,* is for Russian vocal art music what Schubert's *The Linden Tree* is for German vocal art music. In both of them Romantic melodicism is the supreme master. His lyricism is based upon folk song and Italianate devices such as melodic sequences and embellishments. His great contribution to Russian harmony is the frequent use of a diminished seventh chord on the second of fourth degree, a device also used by Tchaikovsky in his Sixth Symphony.[3]

The first major Russian composer was Michael Ivanovitch Glinka (1804-1857). He introduced many important foreign elements into Russian music. From Italy he brought the style of Vincenzo Bellini (1801-1835), and Gaetano Donizetti (1797-1848); from Spain the exotic interest in Spanish rhythms and color; and from Berlin, where he studied with one of Mendelssohn's pupils, Siegfried Dehn (1799-1858), he brought the Mendelssohnian style of orchestration. He also continued Bortniansky's efforts to harmonize Russian chants, a project which was later taken up by Tchaikovsky. His first opera, *A Life for the Tsar,* or *Ivan Susanin,* as it is now known, is a part of the tradition established by Peter the Great of writing music in praise of the tsar. His choral writing in this opera prepared the way for Mussorgsky's *Boris Goudonov.* Another opera, *Russlan and Ludmilla,* established a tradition of combining Russian and exotic clements.

A further contribution was made by Alexander Sergeivich Dargomijsky (1813-1869), who developed a recitative based upon Russian speech elements in his operas *The Stone Guest* and *Russalka.*

THE MAINSTAY OF MUSICAL NATIONALISM—"THE MIGHTY FIVE"—TEAM COMPOSERS (1850-1900)

Originally, these five men were nonmusicians who were taking up the cause of national music. Their organization into a group was helped by the Russian aristocrat, Alexander Dmitrievich Oulibishev.[4] In the course of his work on the biographies of Mozart and Beethoven he had his private orchestra of serfs perform the works of these composers and engaged Mili Alexevic Balakirev (1837-1910), as conductor. Balakirev's leadership and inspiration produced a circle of friends who were later known as the Mighty Five, "The Innovators," or "the Young Russians." The name, "The Mighty Five," which also refers to the five great Slavic nations, was originally applied to these men on the occasion of a program of their music which was performed for the first meeting of the Pan Slavic Committee in 1867.[5] The composers were Balakirev, Alexander Borodin (1833-1887), César Antonovich Cui (1835-1918), Mussorgsky, and Rimsky-Korsakov. They began to work together because they believed that those who have the skill to compose should compose, while those who can orchestrate should orchestrate. Thus Mussorgsky perfected Rimsky-Korsakov's recitative while Rimsky-Korsakov polished Mussorgsky's harmonies and occasionally illogical construction. Rimsky-Korsakov tells of how he, Vladimir Stassov (1824-1906), and Alexander Glazunoff (1865-1936) used to go to Borodin's house after his death to complete any unfinished compositions he might have left.[6] The idea of team writing went so far that the director of the Imperial Russian Opera asked the "Mighty Five" to write a joint work, *Mlada,* an opera-ballet-spectacle that could fully exploit the staging possibilities of the theater in St. Petersburg. Cui, Rimsky-Korsakov, Mussorgsky and Borodin were each supposed to write the first, second, third, and fourth acts, respectively. However, the opera was never performed in this way. Instead, the composers adapted their material to other works.

Balakirev's "Mighty Five" was followed in the eighties by a much larger group of more technically proficient musicians who centered around the famous publisher and patron, Belaiev.

Borodin: Assimilation of Western Classicism and the Folk Music of Greater Russia

Borodin was the most versatile of the "Mighty Five" composers. He achieved a greater assimilation of western musical classicism and Russian nationalism than the others. For example, in the outer movements of his Second Symphony he is faithful to western Classical procedures. The movements are in orthodox sonata form, with exposition, development, and recapitulation. However, his eastern way of developing the themes runs counter to the Classical tradition, in that he reiterates the themes intact while changing the harmonic and orchestral background, rather than fragmenting and reworking the motivic components of the themes.

Rimsky-Korsakov: Toward a Modern Western Sound

Rimsky-Korsakov was the youngest member of the group and was probably the most facile, since he produced the largest quantity of music. There are six basic periods in his writing. During the first, from 1861 through 1872, he established his skill in orchestration. In the second period, 1873 through 1876, he wrote many piano fugues, and studied Tchaikovsky's book on harmony and Bellermann's book on counterpoint. During 1875 through 1886, the third period, he harmonized and published folk songs and wrote operas which are close to the Russian folk idiom. From 1887 through 1896, the fourth period, he completed Borodin's compositions (with Glazunoff's help) and wrote the famous orchestral show pieces *Capriccio Espagnole, Russian Easter Overture,* and *Scheherazade.* In the fifth period, from 1889 through 1896, he adopted the Wagnerian *leitmotif* and the ideas of the *Gesamkunstwerk,* both illustrated in his opera, *Mlada* with its specific stage directions, and in *Sadko.* During the sixth period, from 1897 through 1907, he became more progressive, creating novel harmonies such as those in *The Firebird.*

Mussorgsky: Ethnocentricism and Social Conscience in Music

Mussorgsky is one of the great figures in musical history. There can be no comparison between him and the other members of the "Mighty Five." His nationalism is more humanistic than theirs. He reaches much further into modern compositional techniques. His musical style is very close to the literary style of Dostoevsky. Even his mistrust of technique has a Russian quality. His song cycles, *The Nursery* and *The Songs and Dances of Death,* are prime examples of musical expressionism and illustrate his fondness for irregular meters. *Pictures at an Exhibition* is the supreme example of program music produced with the fewest possible devices.

In *Boris Goudonov,* which he calls a musical folk drama in four acts, Mussorgsky draws upon the Russian opera tradition. The various acts are subdivided into tableaux, not scenes, so the Russian opera-ballet aspect is obvious. The true hero of the drama is the folk and not Boris. The Russian folk song is of great importance in this work. It influences Mussorgsky's melodic and harmonic writing. Melodies occur in which major and minor scales, Russian church modes, pentatonic scales, whole tone scales, and variable scales are used. The harmonization of these melodies often produce consecutive fourths, fifths, and octaves, and unresolved sevenths and ninths—devices which were later used very effectively by Debussy in his Impressionistic music. Music does not exist for its own purpose, according to Mussorgsky. Like speech it is a means of communication. Speech is governed, however, by musical rules while music is human speech itself. The latter quality is shown in Mussorgsky's tremendous capacity of translating inflections of Russian speech into inflections of musical speech.[7] He does this by creating a free flowing musical declamation of a Russian flavor.

Example 1. Mussorgsky, *Boris Goudonov*, Prologue, Scene I.

He was not influenced by Wagner, but he adopted the French "remembrance motive" technique. The orchestral parts are of no great significance. In this work Mussorgsky is essentially a superb Russian vocal composer.

TCHAIKOVSKY: SYNTHESIS OF WEST AND EAST, BYRON AND PUSHKIN

Peter Ilyich Tchaikovsky, founder of Russian symphonic music, established Russian music in the concert halls of the world. Although some of his works are based upon subjective experiences, his style is closer to abstract than program music.

It is easy to misjudge Tchaikovsky's involvement with folk music. We might contrast his middle-class, urban kind of folk music with the music of the peasant as found in Mussorgsky's works. Also, he prefers to smoothe out the natural irregular Russian folk rhythms, presenting them in a more subtle, understated manner, in contrast, for example, to the raw, forceful rhythms of Stravinsky.

His melodic writing is based on the variation technique. He loves to spin out melodies, accompanying them with other melodies. This linear writing should not be identified with counterpoint, but rather with Italian *bel canto* which is embellished through chromaticism.

His harmonic writing tends to be academic and is less original than Chopin's, and less nationalistic than Grieg's. He even wrote a harmony textbook, which achieved success in Germany in a translation by Paul Juon.

In his symphonies Tchaikovsky elaborates on a form which is a combination of the symphonic fantasia (*Romeo and Juliet*) and the standard sonata form. The *Fourth Symphony* is characteristic. The first movement illustrates this combination of fantasia and sonata allegro, the second displays the variation technique, the third uses many orchestral colors and effects, and the fourth is cyclical. Although the entire symphony hinges on the fate motive stated in the introduction, the last movement is the most important. This is not a Finale symphony of Mahler and Bruckner, but there is a strong drive to the last movement, which becomes even more evident in the fifth and sixth symphonies.

At Balakirev's suggestion Tchaikovsky composed the *Manfred Symphony,* a work based upon the play of Lord Byron. He modeled it after Berlioz's *Harold In Italy,* another symphonic setting of the Byronic text. The influence of Berlioz is apparent in *Manfred* which, like *Harold,* is cast into four movements, each bearing a programmatic title. Tchaikovsky also employs the *idée fixe,* although in a different way than Berlioz. While Berlioz absorbs the *idée fixe* into the mood and texture of the work, Tchaikovsky uses the *idée fixe* to dominate and determine the work's character.

It is apparent that Tchaikovsky knew and admired Schumann's setting of Manfred before he wrote his own. This is also indicated by the fact that Tchaikovsky, like Schumann, chose to conclude his setting on a note of religious salvation when there is no hint of salvation in Byron's play. Schumann's setting, however, stresses the melancholy aspects of the drama. His form is loose and fragmentary. Tchaikovsky, on the other hand, is much more dramatic in his treatment and rigid in his structure.

Tchaikovsky's setting of Manfred is probably the most faithful to the nineteenth-century conception of the Byronic hero, a brooding, defiant man of violent conflicts.

Tchaikovsky wrote ten operas. Some are based on national topics, such as *Mazeppa,* with a libretto by Gogol, and some are based upon historical topics, such as *Jungfrau von Orleans,* with a libretto by Schiller. Two, *Eugene Onegin* and *Pique Dame,* are psychological operas in which he goes far beyond his contemporaries. *Eugene Onegin,* subtitled "lyric scenes in three acts," is based upon a versified novel by Pushkin.

Asafiev, a Soviet musicologist, in his "Tchaikovsky's *Eugene Onegin,*" compares the lyrical scenes to the Russian romance, the kind of art song cultivated in the Russian salons.

Tchaikovsky's lyrical scenes do not contain complete romances, however; nor are they the old type of recitative. Instead he uses musical intonations, figures analogous to speech inflections. Russian writers see in the inflection the source, the root that is common to both the sound and the word. Music is a language that is based on intonation. The relationship of each musical work to these intonations is similar to the

Peter Ilyich Tchaikovsky, 1840-1893

George Gordon Byron, 1788-1824

Alexander Pushkin, 1799-1837

relationship that a literary work bears to the language. Musical intonations are best expressed through melody and best carried out by means of melodic sequence. The principle was first used by Glinka.

The introduction to *Eugene Onegin* presents a clear illustration. It is based upon the Tatyana intonation-motive, which is characterized by a fourth that is raised and then lowered again.

Example 2. Tchaikovsky, *Eugene Onegin,* Introduction, Measures 1-3.

This is used many times in the first sixteen measures. The motive is supported by the harmony but it is not the product of it. Further analysis would show that the entire introduction is constructed from the Tatyana intonation-motive.

Suggested Listening Assignments

1. Glinka, Michael: *A Life for the Tsar.* What is characteristic for the choral numbers of this opera? Do they sound like folk songs? What scales does Glinka use?
2. Borodin, Alexander: *Symphony No. 2 in B Minor.* How is the orchestration handled? Can you follow the explanation of his developmental technique as given in the text?
3. Mussorgsky, Modest: *Boris Goudonov.* Listen to one act of this opera. Become aware of the rhythmic flexibility of the vocal parts in accordance with the inflection of the Russian language. Listen for the great variety of scale formations.
4. Rimsky-Korsakov, Nikolai: *The Golden Cockerel.* Listen to the orchestral scintillations. Does he use chromaticism? Enharmonicism? Do you find Oriental and/or Italian melodies?

Suggested Additional Listening Assignments

1. Tchaikovsky, Peter Ilich: *Eugene Onegin.* Can you make out the Tatyana intonation at the beginning? What are the basic differences between the sound of *Boris Goudonov* and *Eugene Onegin*?
2. Tchaikovsky, Peter Ilyich: *Symphony No. 4.* Is this symphony more lyrical than dramatic? Do you find tunes which sound like folk songs or folk dances? In which movements? How are the orchestral colors used in the various movements?
3. Mussorgsky, Modeste: *Songs and Dances of Death.* What kind of melody do you hear? What is the relationship between the vocal and piano parts?

Suggested Reading Assignments

CbT pp. 409-411
EaM pp. 302-317
FdA pp. 518-534
GdA pp. 584-589
HaM pp. 851-875
LpM pp. 944-955
ScO pp. 304-306
UhA pp. 507-518

Suggested Written Assignments

1. Check on the use of folk-like melodies in the 4th, 5th and 6th symphonies of Tchaikovsky.
2. Discuss Rimsky-Korsakov's skill as an orchestrator in *The Golden Cockerel.*
3. Give an account of Tchaikovsky's activities in the United States.
4. Read the life of Mussorgsky. Contrast him and his works with Wagner.
5. Discuss Tchaikovsky's ballet compositions. Relate them to the importance of the ballet in Russia's cultural and musical history.

Footnotes

[1]CaT
[2]LkD, p. 1156
[3]AgT
[4]SvT, p. 15
[5]SvT, p. 109
[6]RnM, p. 238
[7]CbT, p. 409

chapter 14

czechoslovakia: smetana and dvořák

CZECH MIDDLE-CLASS MUSIC

At the close of the eighteenth century Czechoslovakia was a part of the Austro-Hungarian Empire. When Joseph II (between 1780-1790) introduced social reforms which reduced the bondage of the peasants and established some degree of religious tolerance, the rural population moved to the city in great numbers and a strong middle class was established. The nineteenth-century burst of Czech nationalism came from this group. Eighteenth-century Czech aristocrats, such as Count Waldstein, to whom Beethoven dedicated his piano sonata, Opus 53, were enlightened connoisseurs, but musical life was dispersed among widely separated country estates. The new middle class was concentrated largely in the cities, above all, Prague.

With the increasing number of middle-class people coming to Prague, various musical institutions made their appearance there. In 1803 the *Tonkünstlersozietät*, a society of musicians which supported composers and performers and presented concerts and oratorios, was founded. This organization existed up to 1918. In 1808 an association for the raising of musical standards in Bohemia was initiated. In 1811 the famous Prague conservatory was opened and it soon became an important institution for the training of orchestral players.

National and middle-class culture in the Czech cities was further promoted by the composition of music for a great variety of popular dances, an activity which was stimulated in the thirties by the appearance of a new dance, the polka. The polka, which is not Polish in origin, but Czech, competed very successfully with the Viennese waltz.

The youthful Bedřich Smetana (1824-1884) began his career with the composition of polkas for the piano and filled his famous opera, *The Bartered Bride,* with polka-like rhythms.

All this movement toward the establishment of a national and middle-class musical culture occurred in a country where, only 100 years before, one of its greatest musicians had said: "I want to abolish the ridiculous distinction between the national musics."[1] This man was Christoph Gluck, known to us as the great contributor to the music drama of the eighteenth century.

VIENNESE MUSICAL DIALECT

The importance of the new urban middle class, with its desire to equal the aristocracy, is seen in the patronage of operas and of Czech and German *Singspiele,* beginning at the end of the eighteenth century. The popularity of these stage works is also an expression of the desire to imitate Vienna and everything Vienna stood for in music, including the Viennese musical dialect.[2] This dialect, a form of musical nationalism in itself, is known to us by its emphasis on thematic-motivic development. During the entire nineteenth century the power and vitality of this Viennese way of dealing with musical materials imposed itself on European art music, including the music of Czech composers of "national" music. Czech nationalism in the music of Smetana and Dvořák consists of a musical language of Czech flavor spiced considerably with the Viennese musical dialect. Czech nationalism in music thus is actually a Czech-Viennese mixture. The Czech elements are in the foreground but the Viennese musical dialect furnishes the background.

MOZART

Along with the cultivation of the Viennese musical dialect there was in Prague a strong Mozart cult. His operas were performed frequently: the *Abduction from the Serail* (1782), *Figaro* (1786), *Titus* (1791), *The Magic Flute* (1792). *Don Juan,* of course, had its first performance in Prague in 1787. Smetana's *Bartered Bride* was given its first performance in the same theater.

The strong Mozart cult in Prague was perpetuated in the nineteenth century by Jan Václav Tomaschek (1774-1850). He was called the musical "Dalai Lama" of Prague by his famous student, Hanslick. Born and reared in Prague, Hanslick, like so many others, was drawn to the musical flame of Vienna. However, Tomaschek's influence can still be seen in Hanslick's aesthetics in his stand against program music. August

Dance Patterns of the Polka, 1844

Wilhelm Ambros (1816-1876), the writer of an important history of music and a friend of Hanslick in their native Prague, was likewise drawn into the Viennese orbit. Ambros was educated as a lawyer but he was so fond of music that he and Hanslick established their own version of Schumann's *Davidsbündler*: Ambros was "Flamain," and Hanslick was "Renatus," corresponding to Schumann's "Florestan" and "Eusebius."

SMETANA

Smetana and Mozart

Smetana devoted his life to the creation of a truly Czech national idiom, although we also find influences of the Viennese musical dialect and the Prague Mozart cult in his music. His best known work, The *Bartered Bride,* employs some characteristic Mozartean techniques. In fact, it is more of an opera buffa in the sense of Mozart's *Figaro* than a "*Leichte Nationale Operette*," as Smetana labeled it.[3] Its involved plot is typically opera buffa—the bride is sold publicly to the bridegroom—and there is lots of fun and laughter. There are no aristocratic figures in the story; only country folk participate and there is a continual emphasis on dance rhythms that extends even into ensemble settings and recitatives. The quick eighth note motion of the overture is very similar in nature to the opening of Mozart's *Figaro* overture. Likewise, the later canonic counterpoints are strongly reminiscent of Mozart's fugato passages. We are even reminded of Papageno in the stutterings of Vack in the second scene of Act II.

Smetana and the Czech Dance

The prominence of the Czech dance is evident in the first and second subjects of the overture, both of which are anticipations of music in Act II, Scene 6, written to the accompaniment of a syncopated polka rhythm. The entire last scene of Act I is an extended polka. The instrumental number between the first two scenes of Act II is a *furiant,* an older, more indigenous Czech dance. Vacek's number in this second scene has a polka accompaniment, while the duet in Scene 3 is waltz-like and reminds us of "*Leise, leise, fromme Weise*," from *Der Freischütz.* Scene 4 uses a polka rhythm; Scene 6 uses the rhythmic music of the overture's first and second subjects. The famous "Dance of the Comedians," Act III, is still another polka. The whole score is unique in the way in which it successfully combines art and folk music to a degree which was unknown before. There had been some previous attempts at this. For example, the Polish composer, Stanislav Moniuszko

(1819-1872), wrote a folk opera, *Halka* (1844), but his work is performed and appreciated only in Poland. *The Bartered Bride*, on the other hand, because of its combination of Viennese musical dialect and Czech nationalism, has obtained a universal audience.

Smetana and Czech Nationalism

Smetana embodies the spirit of the national awakening in Czech musical life through his many activities as pianist, conductor, and organizer of musical activity. He showed his nationalistic feelings by returning home from a musical post in Sweden after the revolution and devoting his life to his native country. From that point all of his compositions are concerned with musical nationalism through his use of topics and materials which are intimately connected with the geography and history of Bohemia. The symphonic cycle, *Ma Vlast*, is a record of the history of his native land and the places he knew and loved. We may also note his great interest in the common man in such titles as *The Bartered Bride, The Two Widows, The Kiss,* as well as in his historical operas. *Dalibor*, the story of the common man fighting against the king, should be seen in connection with Gerhart Hauptmann's *Florian Geier*, a nineteenth-century drama based on the German peasant revolution of the sixteenth century. *Libeuse*, which Smetana wanted performed only on occasions of national celebration, is the legendary story of a princess who married a peasant. Some of his operas show Wagnerian influence. *Dalibor*, for instance, uses the *leitmotive* technique, but the national element is still more important than the Wagnerian device. Actually, although Smetana greatly revered Wagner, the German's effect on his music was minimal.

DVOŘÁK

Dvořák, the Spielmann (the player-composer)

Dvořák represents the next generation. Since the political situation in Czechoslovakia by that time was relatively more settled and more liberal, his nationalism had other purposes and goals. His father was a butcher and his background is that of the common man. Like Smetana and so many other Czech and Russian composers, he was self-taught. His first years in Prague were spent as a member of a dance band and as a violist in the opera orchestra. From these activities he acquired an intimate acquaintance with folk and popular theater music which remained a strong influence upon him throughout his life.

It is in this experience that we find the basis for the importance of the *Spielmann*, or practical performing-composer, in Dvořák's work.

Many of the finest instrumental performers in the history of modern Western music were native Czechoslovakians, the most notable, perhaps, being the members of the famous Mannheim orchestra. Dvořák's long experience and high degree of skill as a *Spielmann* shows itself in his ability to write for any market. In England he became Victorian society's favorite composer of oratorios; in America he used spirituals in the *New World Symphony.*

One result of his *Spielmann's* attitude was that he became the darling of the music publishers. In addition to Czech music he wrote Pan-Slavic music, based on borrowings of music from friendly Slavic countries. Thus we have his opera, *Wanda,* based upon a Polish topic, and the opera, *Dimitri,* based upon a Russian subject, which incidentally created great difficulties for him.

The development of his style can be studied in the *Slavonic Dances.* The early ones are, quite literally, folk music. Later, more stylized music forms, even Polish mazurkas in the manner of Chopin, appear. The last ones reveal the symphonic influence of Brahms. A characteristic of all of the dances is that each one is really a suite of dances, an organization very similar to the Viennese waltz.

Dvořák, the Symphonist

As a symphonist we can place him in the last of Paul Bekker's three divisions of symphonic style: (1) middle German; (2) program symphonists; (3) Austrian symphonists. It is appropriate to apply Bekker's remarks on the Austrian symphonists to Dvořák:[4]

> The Austrians were superior to the others first of all through their naive joy in just making music (the Spielmann concept) . . . In place of human beings whose sense of tradition and whose personalities formed the center of the Beethoven intellectual and emotional life, came nature with its wonders and mysteries, its inexhaustible and eternal charm, its deep mysticism, touching on the original source of religious feeling. This acquiring of new symphonic building material was necessary in order to find a new structure.

In the *Symphony in G Major,* No. 4, Op. 88, for example, the national element is revealed in subjects that sound like folk songs. In the first movement the first subject is modal and the second subject is very much like a folk dance tune. Key centers underline the folk style: G minor, then G major. The second movement likewise gives us C minor, then C major; the third movement G minor, then G major; and the last G major, C minor, and G major. This shows the greatest simplicity and utmost symmetry. There is an absence in this symphony of a dominant harmonic feeling. To make it still more anti-Viennese, anti-developmental, anti-Beethovian, the symphony is cyclical throughout. The subjects of the first and fourth movements employ the same triadic figure and quote it in the same key:

Example 1. Dvořák, *Symphony No. 4,* First Movement, Measures 18-19.

Example 2. Dvořák, *Symphony No. 4,* Fourth Movement, Measures 26-27.

A similar triadic feeling is found in the first subject of movement one, quoted above, and the coda subject of movement two:

Example 3. Dvořák, *Symphony No. 4,* Second Movement, Measures 132-133.

Furthermore, the first and second subjects of Movement II are related to the first subject of Movement III:

Example 4. Dvořák, *Symphony No. 4,* Second Movement, Measures 1-3.

Example 5. Dvořák, *Symphony No. 4,* Second Movement, Measures 37-39.

Example 6. Dvořák, *Symphony No. 4,* Third Movement, Measures 1-3.

This symphony, harmonically static and very melodic, is characteristic of Dvořák and the *Spielmann's* attitude. It represents harmonic simplicity in a tightly organized structure, with emphasis on folk elements.

Suggested Listening Assignments

1. Smetana, Bedřich: *Bartered Bride Overture.* What is the form of this lively piece? What are its Czech ingredients?
2. Smetana, Bedřich: *From Bohemia's Groves and Meadows.* Listen for the programmatic implications in this work.
3. Dvořák, Antonin: *Symphony No. 4,* Opus 88. Listen for the devices explained in the text.

Suggested Additional Listening Assignments

1. Dvořák, Antonin: *Symphony No. 5,* Opus 95. How does the composer link some of the movements with each other? In which movements does he employ sounds from the "new world"?
2. Smetana, Bedřich: *String Quartet in E Minor.* Do you find traces of Slavic music? Listen for the programmatic qualities of the last movement.
3. Dvořák, Antonin: *String Quartet,* Opus 96. How does Dvořák use the principle of thematic transformation? What major forms are used in the four movements?

Suggested Reading Assignments

EaM pp. 296-302
FdA pp. 535-537
GdA pp. 589-590
HaM pp. 876-887
LpM pp. 955-958
UhA pp. 518-522

Suggested Written Assignments

1. Compare Smetana and Dvořák with respect to their nationalism and their significance in the history of Slavic and Western music.
2. Make a list of Czech (or Slavic) compositions which use the polka rhythm.
3. Look into Dvořák as a composer of sacred music. Write about his smaller works or about his *Stabat Mater.*
4. What place do Dvořák's *Slavonic Dances* have in the world of art and popular music?

Footnotes

[1]TjS, p. 20
[2]AtE, p. 172
[3]TjS, p. 46
[4]BpG, p. 15

chapter 15

poland: chopin

POLISH ELEMENTS

The Polonaise

Chopin's music represents a unique phenomenon in the history of music. His solidly homogenous style has many derivative sources. Some of these are readily traceable while others are extremely elusive. Yet his style is so totally individual and consistent within its own sphere that it is completely inimitable. His most astonishing feature is the incredible variety of contrasting sources, which nothing less than genius could weld into a consistent whole.

The most important of these source materials are the various dance forms which Chopin took over from many different social groups of nineteenth-century Poland and recast them into salon pieces. Of these, the familiar Polonaise represented the music of the highest class of landed aristocracy in Poland, the nobility, who had for centuries dominated the political life of Poland, and lived in large castle-estates. The old aristocratic Polonaise was a slow processional dance somewhat reminiscent of the Renaissance Pavane, but used in the manner of today's "Grand March" as the opener of the evening's entertainment. In the "olden" times it was likely to be ushered through all the halls of the castle and its gardens before giving way to shorter dances such as the courante, allemande, gigue. In this way, the Polish national spirit was given full expression before people embarked upon the fashionable foreign dances. In making a stylization of the Polonaise, Chopin was following the example of a whole generation of composers before him, such as Michael Cleophus Oginski (1765-1833), who had been transferring the aristocratic dance forms into patriotic miniatures for the piano "to delight the ladies." Chopin's works, however, effected an amazing revision of the form. Still working within the salon-piece framework, he imbued it with a highly dramatic and subjective expression that was also patriotic in the fervor of its impelling drive. It approaches the concerto in the scope of the exhibitionistic aspects of its technical brilliancy, yet it never violates the essential dance rhythms or forms. Furthermore, Chopin was always insistent that even though the polonaises were not intended for ballroom use, they should be performed in the original stately tempo, and he had his students think the triple-measure rhythm in six full beats. Many of Chopin's contemporaries were inclined to orchestrate the polonaises. This is an act which would never have even occurred to Chopin with his thoroughly pianistic nature, but it is highly significant of the nature of other composers' changed view of the form as a salon piece.

The Waltz

The waltz represents the music of the lesser Polish nobility, the social class to which Chopin's mother belonged. This social group possessed small landed estates and enjoyed many aristocratic privileges, except for the politically all-important one of conscripting armies. It tended to cultivate strong family ties and patriarchial solidity of a deep enough nature to engender occasional family feuds. Within this tight social structure, there was a great deal of dilettantism in the arts and sciences, and the waltz was a favorite dance symbolic of a polished gentility and decorous mannerism. In Chopin's waltzes, evidences of a lingering closeness to the soil remain very similar to British landed gentry, and can be identified sometimes only in a characteristic turn of a phrase or a melodic habit. Frequently, however, the waltzes exhibit the pervasive stress and dwelling on the second and third beat of the measure so characteristic of the Polish peasant dances. The waltzes fall into two general classes, the *Valses Brillantes* and the *Valses Nobles.* Those waltzes belonging to the *Brillante* class are Opus 18, Op. 34 Nos. 1 and 3, Op. 42, Op. 64 No. 1, and the Posthumous e minor; all others are *Nobles.*[1]

The Mazurka

The Mazurka represents the waltz form of a still lower group of the Polish gentry, the group who had acquired freedom from peasant bondage through extraordinary meritorious service to their lords, but whose land holdings were comparatively small. The gentry were at the lowest rung of the aristocracy, but were by no means in the condition of the mass of the Polish peasantry, who lived in a state of even greater oppression than the Russian muzhik. The Mazurka originated in peasant dance customs; it had gradually infiltrated to the lesser nobility, where it became a favorite of the young people. In Chopin's time it was danced by young people of all classes, and after Russia's conquest of Poland, it even found its way into the salons of St. Petersburg. Perhaps the reason that it remained a "young people's" dance is that it originally required much time, space, and energy. The steps demanded vigorous motion, and a complete "set" of dances lasted a full hour, starting as a group dance, then breaking up into solo dances by specific couples alternating with the group dance. Repetitions of the group episodes were sometimes done to variants known as the *Oberek* and *Kouiaviak.* One Mazurka was danced before midnight, and another at dawn, and the latter was called the "white" mazurka. While Chopin's idealizations of the mazurka have little to do with these ballroom practices, the characteristic rhythms and episodic structures remain. In the following example, there is a characteristic alternating shift of accents between the first and second beats.

Example 1. Polish popular song.

Chopin's mazurkas follow the example of many popular ones in being constructed in motives of short time values and small melodic intervals, often literally repeated at the same or differing pitch levels and accompanied by ostinato figures. Typical of this is the following example:

Example 2. Chopin, *Mazurka*, Op. 7, No. 1.

Other Polish Elements

Polish elements in Chopin's music are evident not only in the stylization of dance forms, but also in the characteristic usages of scale patterns, harmonies, and forms that pervade his works. There are many passages of mixed major-minor tonality, and many melodies founded upon a pentatonic basis, as well as melodies in modal formations. It is characteristic of Chopin to mix these devices freely within a single composition, boldly juxtaposing for a very telling effect. It is perhaps most important to point out that the origin of most of these juxtapositions lies in the result of melodic turns of phrase so characteristic of Polish instrumental melodies. This kind of borrowing is carefully documented by Sofia Lissa in an article, "Nationalism in Romantic Music,"[2] where she gives corresponding examples of melodies with skips of thirds, fourths, sevenths, and ninths which reveal some striking similarities. In addition, Chopin made extensive use of characteristic Polish ornamentations, incorporating them into the pianistic patterning of the art music of France and Italy. It is in the waltzes that these mixtures become the most apparent, and it is this feature above all that makes them so very distinctive. Some of the Nocturnes exploit this feature to some degree, such as Op. 15, No. 2.

CHOPIN AND MOZART[3]

From this it should not be inferred that Chopin merely strove for characteristic Polish idioms and tried to set them down on paper as a sort of ethnological curator. Quite to the contrary, he was educated in the German tradition, particularly in his early years, so his technique was basically that of a west-European style. To this he added his own nationalistic elements. Furthermore, his earliest exposures were to a number of German composers who were uncharacteristically German in their Italian orientation. The most prominent of these was Mozart. The influence of this one master on Chopin's work has hardly been adequately assessed. For instance, when Chopin was in Vienna, many entries in his diary refer to Mozart and Rossini, but there is not a single reference to Beethoven. As a matter of fact, he was one of several important composers including Debussy & Ludwig Spohr (1784-1859), who accused Beethoven of having no taste. It is not surprising to find that Chopin's first composition was a set of variations on an Italian "La ci darem" theme by Mozart, or to find that Mozart's *Requiem* was requested to be sung at his funeral. Actually, the Mozartian style was currently enjoying considerable vogue in Chopin's circle of acquaintances, and his most distinguished music teacher, Joseph Xavier Elsner (1769-1854), had many Mozartian features in his personal style. This was also true of Chopin's contemporaries, Oginsky and Karl Kurpinski (1785-1857), the latter of whom was conductor at the Warsaw opera and composer of twenty-four operas. Indeed, it was Kurpinski who re-orchestrated Mozart's *Requiem* for the funeral of Czar Alexander I, adding piccolo, flutes, oboes, clarinets, and horns to the *Dies Irae,* harps to the *Benedictus,* and brass instruments to the final chorus. Delacroix, the famous French painter and one of Chopin's closest Parisian friends, felt an affinity to Mozart, and declared him to be the Romantic *par excellence.*

After comparing him to Raphael, Delacroix contrasted Mozart with Beethoven, whom he considered savage and uncontrolled, and concluded with the statement, "It is Mozart who unifies in himself this delicate sadness with a serenity and facile elegance of spirit which also has the good fortune to see the pleasant side (of life) as well."[4] Actually, this totality of perception of only the Italianate side of the German styles led Chopin into rather unstable judgments about German composers in general. He was known to have often called Friedrich Kalkbrenner (1785-1849) "the first pianist of the world," and to have classified Meyerbeer as "an immortal composer."

CHOPIN'S ZAL

Liszt's essay on Chopin devotes considerable space to the development of the idea that Chopin was an excellent representative of the national Polish quality known as *zal*.[5] Liszt defined *zal* as a behavior pattern exhibiting emotionalism that was capable of the extremes of emotion, revolt, meanness, and vengeance, and yet on the other hand also capable of the most touching tenderness, patience, and subservience. He said it was the ability of a Pole to cry out in the midst of extreme merriment "Sadness has overtaken me!"[6] This unaccountable melancholy, the kind of *Weltschmerz* which is found in Goethe's *Werther*, as also in the writings of Chateaubriand, Byron, and especially in the aphorisms of Leopardi, is certainly not exclusively Polish, for it was cultivated particularly in Paris. One of the proofs of the universality of *zal*, that it is not confined to the Slavic races, is given by Tiersot in his biography of Smetana where he shows that the principal theme of Smetana's *Moldau*, a theme laden with *zal*, is identical with a melody in a Neapolitan canzonette. Actually, *zal* was a contemporary form of melancholy, expressive of the Romantic movement in general but with little or no definable nationalistic roots. Chopin's F Major Ballada No. 2 is an excellent example of the two-sided *zal* mood, with its tender and wistful aspect of the *Presto con fuoco* which follows. Similar stormy sections occupy the middle section of many of the nocturnes; the tempestuous side alone is represented by the *Polonaise* in F-sharp major—a work which also illustrates the integration of various forms within a larger form.

CHOPIN AND FRANCE

While today we are very much apt to look for the Polish elements of Chopin's style, his contemporaries tended to think of him as a Frenchman, and quite specifically as a Parisian salon composer. Despite his strong nationalistic tendencies, typified by his desire that his heart be buried in Poland, Chopin might possibly have acknowledged his French allegiances. His ancestry on the paternal side went back to a Lorraine family, and his upbringing as a lesser aristocrat in Poland was an excellent basic training for what he would have considered the fountainhead of gracious and elegant living—Paris. It speaks most eloquently of him that once having resided in Paris, he never again felt quite at ease anywhere else, whether at Nohant, London, or Majorca, and that indeed he became a true adoptive Frenchman, never again to return to his homeland.

A concrete French influence upon Chopin appears in his application of the France *Romance*. Every composer residing in Paris wrote romances regardless of his nationality: Gossec, André Grétry (1741-1813), Spontini, Jean François Lesueur (1760-1837), (teacher of Berlioz), Cherubini—it was the accepted thing to do. Thus Bizet inserted romances in his operas, and even Wagner wrote one to a text by Béranger entitled "The Farewell of Mary Stuart to France." The texts of the romances were in accordance with the growing militaristic sentiments of the times. In later times German youth would cultivate some of these tunes to found a whole new literature of military guard songs. Classifiable by their texts, the French romances were either sentimental and touching upon the tender and melancholic chivalric, and tending toward the military, the dramatic, or dedicated to the concept of the "night." Musically, they occupied a position analogous to the *air de cour* of baroque times. They were usually structured in stanza form prefaced by an introductory recitative, and incorporating a refrain. The recitatives are unquestionably the origin of Chopin's *quasi recitative* introductions such as one found at the beginning of the Ballade in G minor, and their melodic turns often find echoes in his melodies.

CHOPIN AND BEL CANTO[7]

At the time, Paris was enjoying a wave of enthusiasm for things Italian, not only in the antiquarian sense, as was exhibited in the popularity of the "*Grand Tour*," but also in the operatic and vocal music forms. Stendahl's famous work on Rossini exemplified the strength of fervor in the current vogue, and the last chapter of a music history by Kiesewetter is entitled "Beethoven and Rossini." It was not just the French who were considering Rossini an immortal but the Russians and Germans as well.

Out of this current wave, Chopin eagerly imbibed the Italian *bel canto* lyrical intoxicants. In this he was by no means an innovator, for Muzio Clementi (1752-1832), Liszt and Kalkbrenner had already set some of the Romantic traditions by adapting the *bel canto* to keyboard idioms. Principal among these was the idea of moving the listener through the beauty and charm of the melody alone. This was accompanied by an increased interest in periodic construction analogous to strophic formations and adoption of the pervasive *da capo* structure. In its final stages, *bel canto* had led to the treatment of the human voice as an instrument of the greatest agility. Similarly, Chopin was to transfer the vocal qualities to the keyboard, forging the very utmost of "singing" possibilities from an essentially percussive instrument.

Various aspects of Chopin's style show the influence of *bel canto.* The most notable is his preference for monody with skeletal accompaniment. Even when he did write contrapuntally, it was essentially a free counterpoint, reminiscent of the duet techniques rather than of genuinely polyphonic structure. Such an emphasis upon melody was bound to affect form and construction, instituting a preference for the shorter forms that allow melodic domination and do not require developments as, for example, sonatas and concertos. The Italian influence is also revealed in a regular scheduling of period and phrase structure that is comfortably predictable after the enunciation of the first pattern line, even when couched in irregular groupings. The almost consistent use of *da capo* forms is surely a *bel canto* influence, as is the type of arabesque exhibited in the famous Nocturne in E-flat. Frequent use of parallel thirds and sixths and a fondness for the Neapolitan sixth chord also constitute additional Italianate influences.

John Field is generally conceded to be the transmitter of Clementi's influence to Chopin. From this, it should not be assumed that Clementi was instrumental in the formation of the Nocturne form. Neither should it be assumed that Bonifacio Asioli (1769-1832), founder of the Milan Conservatory, furnished the original model through the vocal "nocturnes" he was known to have composed in the Napoleonic era. The Nocturnes of both Field and Chopin are derived rather from a type of French romance, the *chanson nocturne,* which incorporated texts dedicated to the night. These compositions were usually for two equal voices in parallel thirds and sixths, cast in an ABA form, with the B section serving as a trio in the minor mode. Published as sheet music, the title pages usually bore a vignette portraying a young woman, alone and intensely contemplative in the moonlight, seated in the ruins of an old castle. They were produced in great quantity and enjoyed tremendous popularity with all social classes, so their influence upon Field and Chopin cannot be overlooked.

Suggested Listening Assignments

1. Chopin, Frédéric: *Ballade No. 2 in F Major, Opus 38.* Can you hear the *zal* quality? The melancholy? The tempestuous emotions?
2. Chopin, Frédéric: *Waltzes.* Listen to any one of the waltzes. Can you hear the mixed tonalities Chopin uses? What kind of ornamentation does Chopin prefer?
3. Chopin, Frédéric: *Mazurka, Opus 7, No. 1.* How does Chopin treat the short motive in this mazurka? What quality does the bass part have?

Suggested Additional Listening Assignments

1. Chopin, Frédéric: *Polonaises.* What kind of musical expression do you find? What kind of rhythm? How is virtuosity handled?
2. Chopin, Frédéric: *Nocturnes.* Listen to any one. What is the musical form? Can you describe the expressive quality of the middle section of the one you listened to?

Suggested Reading Assignments

CbT pp. 358-360
EaM pp. 213-220
FdA pp. 415-424
GdA pp. 516-519
HaM pp. 808-817
LpM pp. 814-816; 823-825
ScO pp. 281
UhA pp. 466-469

Suggested Written Assignments

1. What are the similarities between a Chopin mazurka, polonaise and ballade?
2. What connection can you find between Chopin's music and the political and social history of Poland?
3. To what extent does Chopin's music represent the music of the rising European middle class?

Footnotes

[1]PbC, p. 73
[2]LzL, p. 100
[3]ZfC, p. 177
[4]ZfC, p. 194
[5]WfM, p. 117
[6]PbC, p. 50
[7]SwL, p. 230
[8]KgM, p. 60
[9]CjD, p. 44

bibliography

The following bibliography is selective, representing however a broad coverage of sources and containing materials in foreign languages as well as in English. In addition, an effort has been made to include articles and books of fairly recent publication. The abbreviations which appear with some of the items are derived from the first letter of the author's last name, the first letter of his first name, and the first letter of the first word of the work's title. For example, Paul Henry Lang's *Music in Western Civilization* is abbreviated LpM. These abbreviations are used only with those publications which have been cited in the footnotes or in the reading assignments at the end of each chapter.

Abraham, Gerald, *Borodin: The Composer and His Music.* London: Reeves, 1927.

——, *Chopin's Musical Style.* London: Oxford, 1946.

——, *Rimsky-Korsakov.* London: Duckworth, 1945.

——, *Schumann: A Symposium.* London: Oxford University Press, 1952.

——, *Studies in Russian Music.* New York: Scribner, 1936.

——, *The Music of Tchaikovsky.* New York: Norton, 1946.

AtB Adorno, Theodor W., "Bilderwelt des Freischütz," *Moments Musicaux,* Frankfurt: Suhrkamp, 1964.

AtE ——, *Einfuhrüng in die Musiksoziologie.* Frankfurt: Suhrkamp, 1962.

——, *Versuch über Wagner.* Frankfurt: Suhrkamp, 1952.

AgT Assafjew, B. W.-Glebow, *Tchaikovsky's "Eugene Onegin."* Potsdam: Athenaion, 1948.

Barzun, Jacques, *Berlioz and the Romantic Century.* Boston: Little, Brown, 1950.

——, *Classic, Romantic and Modern.* Boston: Little, Brown, 1961.

BpG Bekker, Paul, *Gustav Mahlers Sinfonien.* Berlin: Schuster & Loeffler, 1921.

———, *The Story of the Orchestra.* New York: Norton, 1936.

Brion, Marcel, *Schumann and the Romantic Age,* translated by Geoffrey Sainsbury. New York: Macmillan, 1956.

Brown, Maurice, J. E., *Schubert: A Critical Biography.* New York: The Martin's Press, 1958.

Bücken, Ernst, *Die Musik des 19. Jahrhunderts bis zur Moderne.* Potsdam: Athenaion, 1928.

Calvocoressi, M. D., *Modest Mussorgsky: His Life and Works.* Fair Lawn, N. J.: Essential Books, 1956.

CbT Cannon, Beekman C., Alvin H. Johnson, and William G. Waite, *The Art of Music.* New York: Crowell, 1960.

CrS Capell, Richard, *Schubert's Songs.* New York: Macmillan, 1957.

Carse, Adam, *The History of Orchestration.* London: Paul, Trench, Trubner & Co., 1925.

———, *The Orchestra from Beethoven to Berlioz.* Cambridge: Heffer, 1948.

CaT Cherbuliez, Antoine E., *Tchaikovsky und die russische Musik.* Zürich: Müller, 1948.

CjD Chominski, Jozef Michal, "Die Evolution des Chopinschen Stils," *The Book of the First International Congress devoted to the Works of Frederick Chopin,* Warszawa: Polish Scientific Publishers, 1963.

Cooper, Martin, *French Music from the Death of Berlioz to the Death of Fauré.* New York: Oxford, 1951.

CfZ Czokor, Franz Theodor, *Zeuge einer Zeit. Briefe aus dem Exil, 1933-1950.* Munich: Langen-Müller, 1964.

Demuth, Norman, César Franck. London: Dobson, 1949.

Deutsch, Otto Erich, *Schubert: A Documentary Biography.* London: Dent, 1946.

Doernberg, Erwin, *The Life and Symphonies of Anton Bruckner.* London: Barrie and Rockliff, 1960.

Donington, Robert, *Wagner's Ring.* London: Faber and Faber, 1963.

Dumesnil, René, *La musique romantique française.* Paris: Aubier, 1944.

EuF Eckart-Bäcker, Ursula, *Frankreichs Musik zwischen Romantik und Moderne.* Regensburg: Bosse, 1965.

EaM Einstein, Alfred, *Music in the Romantic Era.* New York: Norton, 1947.

———, *Schubert: A Musical Portrait,* translated by David Ascoli. New York: Oxford University Press, 1951.

EeB Esteve, Edmond, *Byron et le romanticisme français.* Paris: Hachette, 1907.

FdA Ferguson, Donald N., *A History of Musical Thought,* 2nd ed. New York: Appleton-Century-Crofts, Inc., 1948.

Gal, Hans, *Johannes Brahms: His Work and Personality,* translated by Joseph Stein. New York: Knopf, 1963.

Geiringer, Karl, *Brahms: His Life and Work,* translated by H. B. Weiner and Bernard Niall. New York: Oxford University Press, 1947.

Glinka, Mikhail, *Memoirs,* translated by Richard B. Mudge. Norman: University of Oklahoma Press, 1963.

GdA Grout, Donald Jay, *A History of Western Music.* New York: W. W. Norton & Co., Inc., 1960.

Harding, James, *Saint-Saens and His Circle.* London: Chapman and Hall, 1965.

HaM Harman, Alec, and Wilfrid Mellers, *Man and His Music: The Story of Musical Experience in the West.* New York: Oxford University Press, 1962.

HaS Hutchings, Arthur, *Schubert.* London: Dent, 1945.

Jacob, Heinrich Eduard, *Felix Mendelssohn and His Times,* translated by Richard & Clara Winston. Englewood Cliffs, N. J.: Prentice-Hall, 1963.

Jacobs, R. L., "Schumann and Jean Paul," *Music and Letters,* 30:250-258, 1949.

KgM Knepler, Georg, *Musikgeschichte des 19. Jahrhunderts, Vol. I.* Berlin: Henschel, 1961.

Kracauer, S., *Orpheus in Paris: Offenbach and the Paris of His Time.* New York: Knopf, 1938.

Landormy, Paul, *Gounod.* Paris: Gallimard, 1942.

LpM Lang, Paul Henry, *Music in Western Civilization.* New York: Norton, 1941.

LkD Laux, Karl, "Das 19. Jahrhundert-Russland," *Musik in Geschichte und Gegenwart,* edited by Friedrich Blume, XI, 1156-1168. Kassel: Bärenreiter, 1963.

Leyda, Jay (ed.), *The Mussorgsky Reader,* translated by Jay Leyda and Sergei Bertensson. New York: Norton, 1947.

LzL Lissa, Zofia, "Le style national des oeuvres de Chopin," *Annales Chopin,* Vol. 2.

LaD Lorenz, Alfred, *Das Geheimnis der Form bei Wagner.* Berlin: Max Hesse, 2 vols., 1924.

Martin, George, *Verdi: His Music, Life, and Times.* New York: Dodd, Mead, 1963.

Mellers, Wilfrid, *Romanticism and the 20th Century.* London: Rockliff, 1957.

Menstell Hsu, Dolores, "Carl Maria von Weber's Preciosa: Incidental Music on a Spanish Theme," *The Music Review,* 26:97-103, 1965.

MdS Mintz, Donald, "Schumann as an Interpreter of Goethe's Faust," *Journal of the American Musicological Society,* 14:235-256, 1961.

MhG Moser, Hans Joachim, *Geschichte der Deutschen Musik.* Stuttgart: Cotta, 1924.

Newman, Ernest, *The Life of Richard Wagner.* New York: Knopf, 1933-46, 4 vols.

———, *The Unconscious Beethoven.* London: Parsons, 1927.

Newmarch, Rosa Harriet, *The Music of Czechoslovakia.* London: Oxford, 1942.

Piston, Walter, *Harmony,* third edition. New York: Norton, 1962.

Plantinga, Leon B., *Schumann as Critic.* New Haven: Yale University Press, 1967.

PbC Pozniak, Bronislaw von, *Chopin*. Halle: Mitteldeutscher Verlag, 1949.

Radcliffe, Philip, *Mendelssohn*. London: Dent, 1954.

RmJ Reimann, Margarete (ed.). *Johann Mattheson, Der vollkommene Kapellmeister*. Kassel and Basel: Bärenreiter, 1954.

RnM Rimsky-Korsakov, Nikolai Andrevich, *My Musical Life*, translated by Judah A. Joffe, third revised edition. New York: Knopf, 1942.

Robertson, Alec, *Dvořák*. London: Dent, 1945.

Rolland, Romain, *Musicians of Today*. New York: Henry Holt and Co., 1915.

ScO Sachs, Curt, *Our Musical Heritage*, second edition. New York: Prentice-Hall, 1955.

Salazar, Adolfo, *La Música en La Sociedad Europea. El siglo XIX*, Tomo II., IV. Mexico: El Colegio de Mexico, 1946.

SwB Salmen, Walter (ed), *Beiträge zur Musikanschauung im 19. Jahrhundert*. Regensburg: Bosse, 1965.

SwL Sandelewski, Wiaroslaw, "Les éléments du 'bel canto' Italien dans l'oeuvre de Chopin," *The Book of the First International Musicological Congress devoted to the works of F. Chopin*. Warszawa: Polish Scientific Publishers, 1963.

Saunders, William, *Weber*. New York: Dutton, 1940.

ShS Schwab, Heinrich W., *Sangbarkeit, Popularität und Kunstlied*. Regensburg: Bosse, 1966.

Searle, Humphrey, *The Music of Liszt*. London: Williams and Norgate, 1954.

SvT Seroff, Victor Ilyitch, *The Mighty Five, the Cradle of Russian National Music*. New York: Allen, Towne & Heath, 1948.

Sessions, Roger, *Harmonic Practice*. New York: Harcourt, Brace & World, 1951.

Shir-Cliff, Justine, Stephen Joy, and Donald J. Rauscher, *Chromatic Harmony*. New York: Free Press, 1965.

Sitwell, Sacheverell, *Liszt*, revised edition. New York: Philosophical Library, 1956.

Stefan, Paul, *Anton Dvořák*, translated by Y. W. Vance. New York: The Greystone Press, 1941.

SjR Stein, Jack M., *Richard Wagner: The Synthesis of the Arts*. Detroit: Wayne University Press, 1960.

Stendhal, pseud. of Marie Henri Beyle, *Life of Rossini*, translated by Richard N. Coe. London: Calder, 1956.

SrH Strauss, Richard (ed.), *Hector Berlioz, Treatise on Instrumentation*. New York: Kalmus, 1948.

SwS Strunk, W. Oliver (ed.), *Source Readings in Music History from Classical Antiquity through the Romantic Era*. New York: Norton, 1960.

Thayer, Alexander Wheelock, *The Life of Ludwig van Beethoven*, revised and edited by Elliot Forbes. Princeton, N. J.: Princeton University Press, 1964.

TjS Tiersot, Julien, *Smetana*. Paris: Renouard, 1926.

Tischler, Hans, "Classicism and Romanticism in Music," *The Music Review*, 4:168-205, 1953.

——, "Mendelssohn Style," *The Music Review,* 8:255-1947.
Tovey, Donald Francis, *Essays in Musical Analysis,* Vol. IV. London: Oxford University Press, 1935-1940.
Toye, Francis, *Giuseppe Verdi: His Life and Works.* London: Heinemann, 1931.
Turner, Walter James, *Beethoven: The Search for Reality.* New York: Doran, 1927.
——, *Berlioz: The Man and His Work.* London: Dent, 1934.
UhA Ulrich, Homer, and Paul A. Pisk, *A History of Music and Musical Style.* Harcourt, Brace and World, Inc., 1963.
Vallas, Leon, *César Franck,* translated by Hubert Foss. New York: Oxford, 1951.
Walker, Frank, *The Man Verdi.* London: Dent, 1962.
Weinstock, Herbert, *Chopin: The Man and His Music.* New York: Knopf, 1949.
——, *Donizetti and the World of Opera.* New York: Pantheon, 1965.
——, Tchaikovsky. New York: Knopf, 1943.
WeM Werner, Eric, *Mendelssohn: A New Image of the Composer and His Age.* New York: Free Press of Glencoe, 1963.
WfM Wührer, Friedrich, *Meisterwerke der Klaviermusik.* Wilhelmshaven, Heinrichshofen, 1966.
ZfC Zagiba, Franz, "Chopin als Mozartverehrer," *Chopin Jahrbuch.* Zürich: Amalthea, 1956.

index